To my children, Aidan and Will.
May your quest for a deeper understanding always enrich you.

ACKNOWLEDGEMENTS

Thanks to all the people who helped make this book possible, but especially Jennifer Siegel, for all her hard work; Eugene Cottrell, for making photos on a national holiday; Aidan Rhode and Annabelle Bartrop, for their help digging clay; all the folks at CCCC, who allowed the images to be created, especially Phil Ashe and Karen Allen; Fiona Holland, for her editorial assistance and general brilliance; Sue Mullroy, for access to kilns and events; Will Rhode, for sleeping enough; all my students, who forced me to make sure that the information I was presenting was clear and accurate; Carol Walborn and Victoria Christen, for helping me get started in clay; my mum and dad, who allowed for such latitude in my life; and to the wise people I have had the honour of working with along the way, thanks for the guidance and the help: Carmen Elliott, Barbara Higgins, Cathy Kiffney, Joanne Andrews, Joe Cole, Emma Skurnik, Ana Howard, and Emily MacFadyen, and every-one else – you know who you are.

First published 2010 in Great Britain by
A&C Black Publishers
36 Soho Square
London W1D 3QY
www.acblack.com

ISBN 978-1-408-11006-5

Copyright © Dan Rhode 2010

All photos, unless otherwise noted copyright © EPiC Photo (Eugene Cottrell).

Published simultaneously in the USA by
University of Pennsylvania Press
3905 Spruce Street
Philadelphia, Pennsylvania 19104-4112
www.upenn.edu/pennpress

ISBN 978-0-8122-2141-1

Book designed by Penny Mills.
Cover design by James Watson.

Cover main image: Doug Dotson, *Bottle*, 2009, 23 x 23 x 23cm (9 x 9 x 9in.). Thrown and altered stoneware, fired to cone 10 in a soda firing. *Photo by the artist.*
Details from other photos credited within the book.

Printed and bound in China.

Contents

Introduction

There are many books available to the person interested in learning the basics of pottery making, but many fall short of giving any more than the briefest of introductions to the methods and equipment used. Using these sorts of books can be fraught with frustration as basic forming, firing or glazing problems arise that are not adequately (if at all) addressed in the text. What the more inquisitive and thorough clay artist needs is a book that provides information about both the basic and somewhat more advanced issues of clay-making in a comprehensive yet easy-to-use format. Many, many books will lead the beginner through the stages of throwing and simple glazing, but in order to succeed in making clay objects, the successful potter needs more than that. That's where this book comes in.

Introducing Pottery: the Complete Guide is just what its title describes: a book that gives a more complete overview of the methods, techniques, equipment and theory behind creating with clay. This book aims to provide the reader with a user-friendly, well-organised source of information that will allow the beginner and more advanced artist to solve problems as they develop and keep improving their skills.

Getting started with clay can be intimidating, while moving into new areas of working can be equally daunting. The sections in this book on throwing, handbuilding and sculpting will allow people with previous experience with clay to develop new skills while taking advantage of their previous experience. Many techniques are illustrated and detailed, and the uses of specialised tools to get specific results are explained. Beginners will find the step-by-step illustrations helpful when making their very first pieces as well. The development of an array of hand-made tools is encouraged to promote personalisation of work.

An in-depth look at glaze making, formulation, application and firing will help most artists move beyond the confines created by a lack of understanding of the basics of how glazes work. Personalising this process helps to make an individual's work stand out. Furthermore, an understanding of the fundamentals of formulation will not only help potters make glazes that are safer and more durable but also aid non-functional artists to go beyond the mainstream 'school use only' glazes to ones that really speak to their aesthetic.

Learning about the differences in firing techniques is important when getting started so that resources are allocated well and a suitable method can be used. The section on kilns provides users basic information on what is required to set up a variety of kilns, and some of the ways of preparing, loading, and firing electric, gas, wood and raku kilns. Firing schedules are included to help ensure success, and theoretical information is included so that users can go beyond the basics and move in the direction that best suits their work. For those that already have some experience, but would like to continue to a more advanced level, encouragement is provided to the would-be professional artist to help them move beyond the safe sphere of their early learning environment to become an entrepreneur and business owner. The book provides information on the first steps to take to start out on your own.

As a practice, working with clay requires patience: patience to learn the skills required in order to achieve specific results, but also patience for the material to go through the changes involved. Clay as a medium *demands* patience on the part of the craftsperson; there is no way to hurry the process, and this is sometimes the part about clay work that draws people in. Additionally, pottery is not an immediate art form, neither in time nor proximity. Whereas the fibre artist sews the fabric, and can see the evolution of their work in their own hands, much of what the clay artist 'creates' happens in a very hot kiln away from prying eyes! This element of chance and mystery involved with making clay enchants many who spend their days shaping this basic material. This book acknowledges these challenges, and promotes ways of taking advantage of clay's intrinsically complex characteristics.

Getting some degree of control over the materials making up clay and glazes is tantamount to success with clay. And knowledge about the make-up of the materials will allow any clay artist to creatively solve problems as they arrive. The information in this book will allow a beginner and more advanced craftsperson to evolve their work in a step-by-step approach, giving them the tools with which to evaluate and learn from their successes and failures. Frustration arises when the mysteries that arise as the work progresses are not able to be evaluated, and this is when people normally give up. One aim of this book is to provide clay artists with enough information so as to not overwhelm but to clarify.

Ultimately, this book provides all the information needed to get the beginner up and running, with the aim of supporting and encouraging those who have just started out. It will then allow them to develop their skills and progress beyond this level to a more knowledgeable stage, while those who have perhaps already started out in classes will find this book a fantastic resource to fill in all the gaps once they have learnt the basics. In short, a book for beginners and beyond.

Making clay objects is a fascinating process; a process fraught with moments of bliss as well as frustration. Having a helpful guide along for the journey is incredibly beneficial. The information provided in *Introducing Pottery: the Complete Guide* is meant to serve in just this way.

1

CERAMIC HISTORY

Venus of Dolní Věstonice, the oldest known fired-clay object, c. 27,000 BC, 11 x 5.5cm (4½ x 2in.). *Used with permission from the Anthropos Institute, Moravian Museum, Brno, Czech Republic.*

Early history

Making pottery is undoubtedly one of the oldest art forms still practised today. Archaeologists estimate clay was first fired by Stone Age hunter-gatherers more than 30,000 years ago, but none of this earliest work survives. A few of the clay figures made by later sculptors have been found, but by and large the earliest work has long since been broken down into its constituent parts by natural forces.

Wholesale pottery making, when it did finally get started, has at its roots a utilitarian need. This need was recognised at different times in different parts of the world. Although not noted as such in historical texts, this development denotes what could be called the 'ceramic age'. The impacts of fired clay on humanity were profound and of no less consequence than those resulting from the discovery of iron or bronze.

Many prehistoric human groups spent their time moving about the landscape in search of the resources they needed to survive. Everything these hunter-gatherer communities owned had to be relatively easy to find, replace, and carry from place to place. Heavy, fragile items such as pottery were therefore not of much use to early humans. At about the time of the end of the last ice age, around 10,000BC, an interesting coincidence appears to have happened: humans began to form more permanent settlements and the first fired-clay storage vessels were created. Whereas hunter-gatherers would have had no need for heavy clay containers, settled groups of early farmers would have had a vital need for a way of storing the fruits of their labour. Chief amongst the enemies of farmers then and now are insects, small mammals and moisture. A leather bag would hardly fit the bill as a decent storage container for very long. Woven baskets would stand up to the test even less well. Lidded clay pots, on the other hand, keep out pests and protect the contents (to some extent) against the weather. Arguably, without fired clay, the development of early humans from hunter-gatherers to early farmers would not have been able to take place.

Significantly, natural clay deposits are often found near fertile areas of soil, areas that would have been sought after by early farmers. River bottoms have a tendency to accumulate rich eroded soils in deep flat expanses, while in other often adjacent areas clay sediments often lie exposed due to the carving action of flood waters. Early human settlements used fire on a daily basis for cooking and heating. Clay from the nearby outcroppings might have been shaped by children, and then thrown into the fire, or the clay under a big fire may have become permanently hardened. Regardless of how the vitrification of clay was discovered, it seems clear that it was discovered in many places around the earth at different times, by various groups of people looking for a solution to the problem of how to store food.

Jōmon pottery

Jōmon pottery is now believed to include some of the earliest examples of humans using clay and fire to create a more permanent form. Early pots date from as long ago as 12,000BC. Some of these pots are highly decorated with wild imagery, while others are plainer and show an

imprint of a rope or fibres, from which the name Jōmon arises; literally, it means rope-impressed.

The Jōmon people lived on what is now the main island of Japan. Although they lived the life of a hunter-gatherer tribe, food and resources are believed to have been so plentiful that moving about to find food was unnecessary. They did not grow crops, but lived off the plentiful food sources available to them in the seas and growing abundantly on land. Predators were unknown to the Jōmon, and archaeologists believe their lives were peaceful and relatively easy. The

pottery they made displays a remarkable level of artistic flair, indicating that their work may have played a bigger role in their ceremonial life than in the daily storage of food. Clearly, some pottery was used for preparing food and for cooking, but other work is so elaborate it is hard to imagine it being used for anything on a day-to-day level.

Increasing amounts of this work are being found today, the discovery and analysis of which will undoubtedly reveal more about this intriguing group. But what we already know is that the Jōmon, living in isolation from other groups of people, continued to make pottery in the same way for thousands of years, firing in bonfires and never developing a kiln. Only when other Asian groups crossed the Yellow Sea did the Jōmon people's technology change.

The Middle East

In the area between the Tigris and Euphrates rivers known as Mesopotamia, in what is now Iraq, early humans found a perfect location for settling down to an agrarian lifestyle. The rivers provided water and excellent soil, along with access to clay. Settlements in this area date back to 8000BC. Here, early pots were made by pinching, paddling and coil-building, but also by pressing clay into baskets and then burning the baskets away.

Pottery was fired in simple, open bonfires. Most people today that work with clay on a regular basis know that a sure-fire way of breaking a big pot into little pieces is to heat it up quickly and unevenly, but those were exactly the conditions available to these early potters. Many of their pots must have broken or cracked. It is likely that many of their broken pots were used in subsequent fires as a buffer or saggar

Jōmon 'Jar', 2500 to 3500BC. Earthenware, handbuilt, bonfire-fired. The meaning of the elaborate patterning found on this vessel is unknown, but archaeologists are generally agreed that it had some kind of ceremonial or ritual significance. ©V&A Images/Victoria and Albert Museum, London.

Mesopotamian Pottery, Painted Beaker, Susa A, late 5th–early 4th millennium BC. Ht: 20.5cm (8 in.). This piece was found in a grave in a large cemetery in Susa in what is now south-west Iran. © *The Trustees of the British Museum.*

Asia

While it is generally believed that some early inventions relating to the firing of clay spread from west to east, from Mesopotamia to Asia, it is also believed that many of the ideas arose spontaneously as early humans evolved from hunter-gatherer to farmer. The earliest pots to be discovered in Asia come from the south-west and date back to about 9000BC. The surviving examples were often buried with the dead or were used as burial urns.

The potter's wheel came into use in Asia relatively soon after it was discovered in the Middle East: the wheel

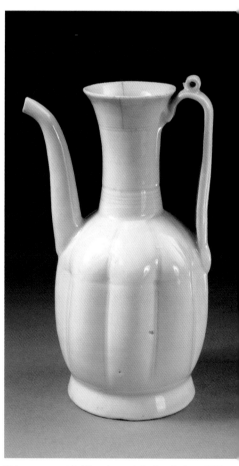

Chinese porcelain 'Ewer', made in Jingdezhen, 960–1127AD. As a town, Jingdezhen dominated the porcelain industry in China for a century. An example of Qingbai ware, this piece was fired in a 'dragon' kiln fuelled with wood in a reducing atmosphere. Highly prized, this type of porcelain was exported around the world from the 11th century. *Photo © V&A Images/Victoria and Albert Museum, London.*

protecting the new pots from the flames. It is also probable that such repeated firings gave these fragments sufficient durability that we are able to unearth them as artefacts today.

Bonfires later evolved into pit fires, which are basically bonfires that have had their air supply choked off by the presence of earth. This serves to slow the firing down, and gave the early potter a chance to control the flow of air by utilising underground tubes. The tubes would be opened up as more fuel was added later in a firing, allowing the temperature to be gradually increased. Pits, of course, fill up with water, so eventually a pit above ground, with a lid, was created: the first updraught kiln. This type of kiln was first seen in the Middle East around 6000BC, but temperatures in the kilns were still well below that needed

to make glass from the materials readily available, so no glazes are found. Instead the pots were burnished to create a denser, polished and slightly more waterproof surface. Oils and plant resins were also used to seal pots against moisture. Most decorations, however, were applied using different-coloured clay, though these would not have been applied to the majority of utilitarian pots used by ordinary people.

It is believed that Mesopotamian potters first used a form of the potter's wheel in about 4000BC. Known as a slow wheel, this took the form of a large flat stone set on a pivot placed on the ground. The stone was often turned by a second person as the first person made the piece. As settlements grew, a pottery industry began to flourish, and advancements continued in both wheel technology and kilns.

A modern day example of maiolica glazing and decorating. Eck and Zeke McCanless, *Elizabeth Mary Devon Bowl,* 2006–2009, 32 x 11.5cm (12½ x 4½ in.). *Photo by Misty Donathan.*

Greece

Greek potters inherited a strong pottery tradition from the Mycenaeans before them. The fast wheel – a wheel that keeps spinning after the force applied to it ceases – was already in use in the area around the Aegean Sea when the classical Greek culture began about 1000BC. During this period pottery was very highly valued and was used extensively during ceremonies and rituals. Pots decorated in slip were produced primarily in Corinth and Athens, where iron-rich beds of clay are readily available. Decorations on the surface of the pots often depict historical

Phiale Painter, Greek 'Vase', made in Athens c. 450–440 BC. Earthenware painted in black slip. An amphora-type vase used to store wine or oil. The area around the figures is painted in slip, leaving the figures showing through. Careful control of the firing process allowed the pot to oxidise, while keeping the iron in the slip reduced to make it black. *Photo © V&A Images/Victoria and Albert Museum, London.*

and the use of cobalt in glazes are believed to be advancements learned by the Chinese from Middle Eastern artisans. In time, however, some of the biggest impacts on world ceramic technologies would come from Chinese kiln advancements. By 1000BC, early Asian potters had achieved the first stoneware temperatures in a kiln. Ash and feldspathic glazes came into use for the first time (although the earliest glazes had been discovered in northern Africa prior to this in the form of Egyptian paste clays).

As updraught anagama ('tube kiln') kilns became prevalent in Asia, firing temperatures increased, and porcelain was being successfully fired during the first thousand years AD. Some of the most prized Chinese porcelains were made during the Song Dynasty from AD960–1279.

Lead was also used as a glaze ingredient from 1000BC (having been borrowed from the artisans casting bronze) as a way of lowering the melting temperature of other materials. However, it was the porcelains exported to the Middle East and later Europe that caught the attention of potters outside Asia. For thousands of years kiln technology throughout the rest of the world lagged behind that of Asia. For hundreds of years, European potters attempted to reproduce Asian porcelains, but their attempts were futile without the necessary materials and kilns. However, their failed attempts were by no means undesirable, and resulted in the creation of majolica, Hispano-Moresque ware, delftware, English delftware, and faience.

events and have a narrative theme. The most prized pots were buried with their owners in graves, and as a result these pots are the ones that have been unearthed most frequently in modern times.

Arguably the most thrilling achievement in ceramics by the Greeks was the ability to control the atmosphere in their updraught, beehive-shaped kilns to create different colours based on the reaction of iron in the pot versus the iron in the slip decoration. The clay in the pot, being less melted, reoxidises more quickly than the iron in the partially melted slip decoration, allowing the pot to end up as an oxidised red-iron colour versus the black-iron colour in the reduced (oxygen-deprived) slip. These pots were fired to about 900°C (1650°F) and there was little if any use of glazes, even though glaze technology was probably known about from work being produced in Egypt. Fine examples of this black-on-red decoration can be seen in many museums today.

North America

While the ability to shape and fire clay into useful forms for human use was discovered in North America sometime around 1000BC, the use of glazes, the potter's wheel and high-temperature kilns was never realised by the early Native Americans. Until the European settlers arrived, bonfires were used to fire clay. Early North American pottery was handbuilt using slabs or coils and decorated with different coloured clays. Various groups throughout what is now the United States began making pottery around the same time. One of the earliest cultures to make pottery extensively was the Hohokam people of what is now Arizona. Around AD500 they were making low-fire pottery decorated with motifs. Some of these designs were painted with coloured clays, others with plant materials following firing. The pottery was used for cooking and for storage of grains harvested from early farming activities.

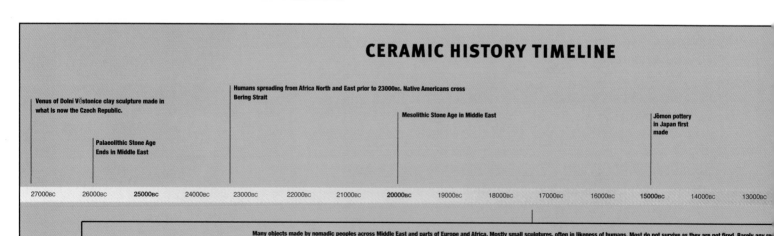

CERAMIC HISTORY TIMELINE

Venus of Dolní Věstonice clay sculpture made in what is now the Czech Republic.

Humans spreading from Africa North and East prior to 23000BC. Native Americans cross Bering Strait

Mesolithic Stone Age in Middle East

Jōmon pottery in Japan first made

Palaeolithic Stone Age Ends in Middle East

| 27000BC | 26000BC | 25000BC | 24000BC | 23000BC | 22000BC | 21000BC | 20000BC | 19000BC | 18000BC | 17000BC | 16000BC | 15000BC | 14000BC | 13000BC |

Many objects made by nomadic peoples across Middle East and parts of Europe and Africa. Mostly small sculptures, often in likeness of humans. Most do not survive as they are not fired. Barely any re

NOTES: Palaeolithic Stone Age is 'Old' stone Age; Mesolithic Stone Age is 'Middle' stone Age; Neolithic is 'New' Stone Age. Pre-history is the time before written accounts of activities (dates vary for each culture). Bronze Age: roughly 3000BC to 1000BC (dates vary for each culture). Iron Age: roughly 750BC to 43AD (dates vary for each culture).

Table 1: Ceramic world history table

	MODERN NAMES FOR THESE AREAS					
	Middle East/ Mesopotamia	Japan	China	England	North America	Egypt
People first arrive	90,000BC	30,000BC	80,000BC	30,000BC	14,000BC	120,000 BC
Neolithic Period (New Stone Age)	7000–3000BC	7000–300BC	7000–3000BC	7000–2000BC	7000BC– AD1492	7000–3000BC
Pottery first made	8000BC	12,000BC	8000BC	4000BC	500BC	7000BC
Bronze Age	2000BC	300BC	3000BC	2000BC	none	3000BC
Iron Age	1200BC	300BC	600BC	750BC	none	2000BC
Stoneware temps first achieved	AD500	AD300	1500BC	AD1666	none	AD500
Glazes first used	1600BC	AD400	1500BC (ash)	AD50 (Romans)	none	4000BC (paste)
Potter's wheel first used	4000BC	3000BC	4000BC	100BC	none	2400BC
Notes	The use of tin-based glazes became prevalent about AD800.	During the last ice age, Japan was connected to the mainland. In about 300BC the Jōmon people were overrun by immigrants – the Yayoi.	Porcelain made by AD700.	Until 6500BC the British Isles were connected to mainland Europe; Romans arrived AD43.	Europeans began arriving in 1492.	Northern Africa was the first place on Earth where ceramic glazes were used.

opposite

above Greek vase, barrel-jug, 7th century BC. Found in a tomb at Gastria. Earthenware, wheel-thrown and painted in black and red on a buff-coloured slip. Ht: 32.1 cm (12½ in.), l: 30cm (11¾ in.).
Photo © V&A Images/Victoria and Albert Museum, London.

below Hohokam Pottery, Sacaton Red-on-Buff Jar, Sacaton Phase, AD 900–1100. Made in what is now central and southern Arizona in the United States. Coil built, bonfire fired, decorated with a slip with a high iron content. *Photo © Pueblo Grande Museum and Archaeological Park.*

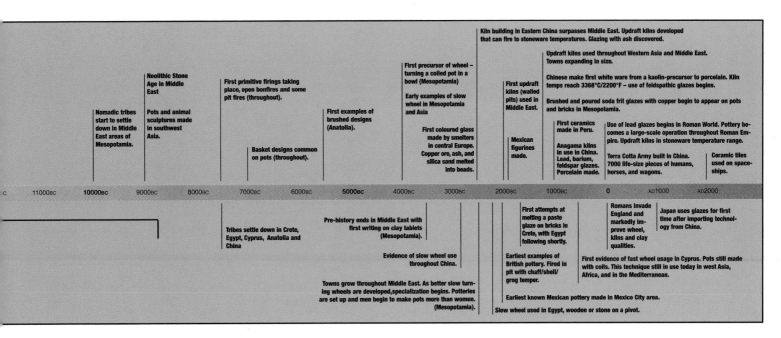

2

CLAY
Geology, Chemistry and Clay Bodies

THE ORIGINS OF CLAY

In the simplest terms, clay is made of rock dust. Natural forces break down various types of rock into powder, and this powder can then be fired in a kiln to become rock-like again. But this time, when it is fired, it might be in the shape of a bowl, mug, plate or sculpture. In return, all the pottery we humans make will someday return to the earth and become part of a mountain to be climbed by our descendants. Pottery is just one stop along the grand mineral cycle taking place on Earth!

The Earth's crust is made of a variety of minerals, primarily oxides, which are combinations of various atoms with oxygen atoms. By far the most common type of mineral is feldspar, a common type of rock. All feldspars of interest to potters contain two main oxides, silica (silicon dioxide) and alumina (aluminium oxide), plus any of a variety of additional oxides. After a profound amount of weathering in nature, the silica and alumina in feldspar become chemically bound to water molecules. Tiny particles of this trio are the basic building blocks from which all clay is derived.

In nature, clays tend to be of two types: primary and secondary. Primary clays are those that have managed to stay relatively close to the rock from which they were sourced. Secondary clays are those that have travelled away from the rocks from which they were created, mainly due to wind and rain blowing or washing them away. Each type of clay has a few identifying characteristics: primary clays tend to have larger particles and tend to be 'purer', i.e. containing fewer impurities such as iron; while secondary clays normally have smaller particles and a greater proportion of impurities picked up as they moved. The most common name given to primary clays used by potters is 'kaolin'. The name often given to secondary clays is 'ball clay', as the fine particles in secondary clay make it sticky enough to form a ball. There are many, many kinds of primary and secondary clays, each with its own characteristics. These clays are collected from many different locations: a mine or quarry, or even someone's back garden. The makeup of the clay will depend on its history, and no two clays will exhibit exactly the same qualities under all conditions.

Rock outcroppings like these will eventually be worn down by natural forces. The tiny bits of rock that wash and blow away may someday be part of a clay artist's creation. *Photo by the author.*

Flowing water moves tiny clay particles around, depositing them when the speed of the water slows down. *Photo by Fiona Holland.*

PROSPECTING FOR CLAY

Ready-to-use clay can of course be bought from suppliers, and this will be discussed later in this chapter (see p.21). But for those looking for a bit more adventure, harvesting wild clay can be rewarding and educational. Depending on where you live, finding clay in your local environment can be very easy or quite difficult. If you know a bit about your local geology, or you have done a bit of gardening, you probably already know something about what you will find in your area. In some places, huge clay deposits lie just under the top layer of soil and vegetation, and digging anywhere will result in finding clay.

Other areas might have several feet of topsoil, which is mainly organic matter, and all of this would have to be removed before clay can be found. Bedrock predominates at the surface in some regions; in other places the ground is almost exclusively sand. If it appears that finding wild clay will be difficult, before giving up, go to a local river or lake and have a bit of a poke around. Put on your boots and, if it is safe, have a bit of a wander up the stream or along the shore and grab handfuls of the substrate.

Sometimes feeling for clay is the best way to find it. Search along the banks, especially in areas where things have been eroded, and look for exposed layers of clay.

Is it clay?

Most people know wet clay when they feel it: it is slippery, slimy and sticky. Perfectly usable clay can be found in its dry state as well, and may not exhibit any of these qualities.

When a potter goes out looking for 'native' or 'wild' clays, there are a variety of tests that can be done to recognise whether a clay is worth harvesting or is better left alone. Reasonably good clay can be identified quite quickly using simple tests.

First, once the clay is wet, try rolling it into a ball. If it sticks and does not crumble, you have found clay with sufficiently small particles to be useful. A further test is to simply roll the clay into a coil with roughly the diameter of a pencil, and attempt to wrap it around your finger. If the clay can do this, you have found a good source relatively free from sand and organic matter, and you can proceed to make things from the harvested clay as it is.

top Sometimes clay can be dug by hand from the ground, usually where exposed by water. *Photo by the author.*
above Dry clay can be harder to identify as being usable clay since it is difficult to test on site. *Photo by the author.*

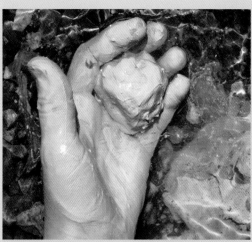

top Rolling a ball of wild clay. *Photo by the author.*
above A simple field test for soft wild clay: if you can wrap it around your finger, it may be plastic enough for making pottery. *Photo by the author.*

Determining firing temperature will be next, and the only way to do that will be to include the clay in your next kiln firing and see what happens. Start with a bisque firing, and work your way up to earthenware and then stoneware temperatures. Be sure only to put a small amount of clay in the kiln at a time, and be sure to put it into a small bowl made of a clay that you know from experience will withstand your test to ensure that any wild clay that melts will be contained.

The colour of the fired clay will normally be determined by the amount of iron found in the clay, and this will also play a role in the clay's melting temperature. Clays high in iron will be darker and will tend to melt at lower temperatures, while lighter-coloured clays will have less iron and will melt at higher temperatures. Wild clays will often melt at fairly low temperatures and may be more suitable for use as either a decorative slip or in a glaze; just substitute your found clay for a portion of the clay in a glaze recipe and see what happens. Another way of making use of wild clay is to wedge it into a higher-temperature 'clay body' (meaning a mixture of ingredients that together make up the clay that you use) to add colour. In this way, as long as you do not add too much, you can still fire to higher temperatures while knowing that some of the clay in your pot was found by you, thus making your pieces a bit more personal.

If you find clay that does not pass the ball and finger-wrap tests, you can often do a little work on the clay yourself to improve its plasticity. With small amounts, you can simply push the moist clay through a screen to remove impurities such as organic matter and sand. For larger quantities, it is best to dry the clay completely, and then re-wet it in a bucket with plenty of extra water to make a thin slurry. This counter-intuitive approach of first drying and then re-wetting takes advantage of a force of nature: completely dry clay that suddenly comes into contact with a lot of water will literally disintegrate and turn into slurry a process called 'slaking'; try watching what happens in a clear plastic cup to a small piece of dry clay when you add water. Conversely, moist clay will do virtually nothing for days while it sits at the bottom of a bucket of water.

Once the clay has slaked, swirl the slurry and allow the mixture to settle for a day or two. Then, either by pouring or scooping, retain just the top half to three quarters of the clay sediment that has settled at the bottom of the bucket. Organic matter will float to the top and can be skimmed off, while the bigger sandy particles will sink to the bottom and can be left behind. If you are careful, there will be no need to sieve the mixture, but if there is a great deal of waste material, it may be necessary.

right From left to right: Cone 10 porcelain, orange high fire stoneware, brown stoneware clay, and red high fire earthenware clay on the bottom. *Photo by Jennifer A. Siegel.*

CLAYS FOR SALE

Industrially produced clays are not often what consumers think they are. In order to achieve a high standard of uniformity with their clay bodies, manufacturers mostly mix their clays from a variety of sources, creating a chemistry in the body that will perform in a particular way. Manufacturers normally do not simply dig some clay out of the ground, clean out impurities, and sell it on. That would be too unpredictable a method, and they would not be able to say with any assurance that the clay would fire reliably to any particular temperature, have certain working properties, or have a reliable fired appearance.

In order to achieve a high level of uniformity manufacturers source the basic ingredients that go into a clay body from several different mines or pits. Often it will be one ingredient from one place, another from somewhere else, and so on. The colouring agents are usually added separately, too, so that colour can be carefully controlled. This also allows the manufacturer to start with a basic recipe and come up with a huge number of different clay bodies. Thereafter, the only difference between two clay bodies might be the amount of colouring agent added to them.

Clay bodies for sale are usually grouped by the temperature or 'cone' (see Chapter 4, p.71 for a description of this term) at which they mature.

Earthenware or terracotta:
low-temperature clays (also known as low-fire clay, see example, right)
(cone 08–1).

Mid-range clays (cone 2–6)

Stoneware: middle to high-temperatures clays (also known as high-fire clay, see example, below) **(cone 6–12)**

right Cathy Kiffney, *Owl Tile*, 2009. 28 x 18 x 1.25cm (11 x 7 x ½ in.). Slab-press mould, red terracotta, decorated with coloured slips and glazes, fired to 1040°C (1900°F). *Photo by the artist.*

below Noah Riedel, *Large Bowl*, 2009. 7.5 x 20 x 20cm (3 x 8 x 8 in.). Thrown and altered stoneware clay, raw-glazed with porcelain slip decoration, single fired to cone 7 in oxidation. *Photo by Seth Tice-Lewis.*

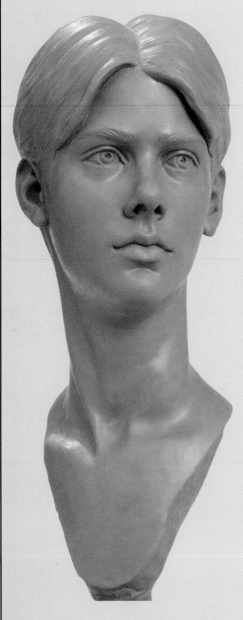

above Dennis Kilgallon, *Wave*, 2004. High-temperature stoneware clay, 59 x 59 x 25.5cm (23 x 23 x 10 in.). The initial model was made in styrofoam, from which a two-piece plaster mould was taken. The piece was then hand-pressed from the mould. When damp, the surface was decorated with sgraffito and incised lines. When dry, the surface was rubbed with a mixture of manganese dioxide and whiting. It was once-fired to cone 11. *Photo by the artist.*

left Susan Draughon, *Andrew Draughon*, 1997, 20 x 46cm (8 x 18 in.). This life-size bust was made from an oil clay called plastilina, and was then used to make a mould from which a bronze was cast. *Photo by Gerry Marketos.*

- Earthenware and stoneware clay bodies come in a wide variety of colour choices (usually earth tones) and textures. The smoother clays are usually sold as clays to be used on the wheel ('throwing clays').

- Coarser clays (which are often just the smooth clays with grog added to them) are usually sold for large thrown or handbuilt pieces, but most clays can be used for a wide variety of projects despite the manufacturers' recommendations.

Other clay bodies include:

- Porcelain: usually a pure white, high-fire clay that is normally very smooth but can also be made coarse through the addition of molochite.

- Paper clays: clays with paper fibres added to increase strength when dry and to reduce the likelihood of cracking while drying.

- Self-hardening or air-hardening: clays that do not require firing to become impervious to water. NB: not recommended for use with food or drinks!

- Raku: clays well suited for the dramatic temperature changes associated with raku firing.

- Oil-based or plasticine: clays that are not fired but instead used to make a mould which is then cast in a foundry.

In many cases the raw ingredients that manufacturers use to make their moist clay bodies are for sale in their dry powdered form. A few artists work to develop their own specialised clay-body recipes, and some manufacturers will mix large batches of these recipes for a fee.

left Jo Bunbury, *Green and Copper Raku Conkers*, 2005, 9 x 8cm (3½ x 3in.). Handbuilt using pinch and coil techniques. *Photo by Martin Avery.*

below left Susan Draughon, *Whale Dreams*, 2006, 20 x 43cm (8 x 17in.). Handbuilt mask from stoneware paperclay, once fired and patinated with bronze patinas and sealed. *Photo by William A. Sosa.*

below right Jennifer Lawler-Mecca, *Amber Lidded Jar*, 2009, ht: 25.5cm (10in.). Thrown and altered, fired to cone 7 in oxidation, decorated with sprigs and cut lines inlayed with slip. *Photo by Randy McNeilly.*

CLAY-BODY CHEMISTRY

Why should anyone care about the chemistry of their clay? Doesn't studying the science behind the artwork take the fun out of it? Absolutely not! The fun comes from being able to do what you want with the material, and understanding the chemistry of clays will provide insight into how to solve problems when things go wrong, and will also open new doors of understanding that allow you to move in new directions. Read through the following sections and see if your clay doesn't take on a new life next time you work with it.

As has been discussed, the theoretical composition of clay is silicon dioxide (commonly referred to as either silica, quartz or flint), aluminium oxide (commonly referred to as alumina), and chemically bound water. This chemical formula for pure dry powdered clay is written as:

$Al_2O_3 \ 2SiO_2 \ 2H_2O$

where Al_2O_3 is the formula for alumina, SiO_2 is the formula for silica, and H_2O is the formula for water.

Alumina has several special properties that make it very important to artists working in clay. First of all, by itself it has a very high melting point, more than 2000°C (3632°F). Generally, this material inhibits the melting of other materials at high temperatures. In its raw state it is a white powder, and it is unaffected by the temperatures reached in normal ceramic kilns. It is added to clay bodies as a component in clays, feldspars, certain frits and in its pure form.

Most people have seen **silica** crystals before, either in the form of inexpensive jewellery or, more likely, in the form of beach sand. Silica crystals are everywhere! They can be found in the rocks used on gravel roads and in rock outcroppings all over the world. Quartz

Some examples of quartz: in pebbles and in strips in a larger rock. *Photos by the author.*

Eck McCanless, *Blue Crystalline Pot*, 2008. Dia: 20cm (8in.). A pot glazed with a macro-crystalline glaze, fired to cone 10. *Photo by Misty Donathan.*

crystals often show up as white sparkles in grey or black rocks.

Typically, crystals form when liquid minerals are cooled slowly, especially in the absence of alumina, this can be seen in the photo above where large zinc crystals have formed in a macro-crystalline glaze. Silica has a high melting temperature of about 1650°C (3002°F); the partially melted silica in a clay body is what holds the piece together. In a clay body, silica is normally added through the clay used, but can also be added through feldspars, frits, talc and wollastonite, as well as in its pure form.

Water in its chemically bound form can be confusing for potters. The clays that ceramicists use have two kinds of water in them until they are fired: the chemically bound kind and the non-chemically bound or 'mechanical' kind. Chemically bound water is locked into the molecular makeup of clay and will not come out through drying. Yes, dry powdered clay contains water molecules, even though it is not wet! Mechanical water is the kind that we add to clay from the sink, or subtract through drying. The chemically-bound kind can only be removed through heating, and once removed the clay becomes a ceramic material and can no longer be re-softened.

Clay-body additives and colourants

Many different kinds of materials can be added to clay bodies to achieve various characteristics depending on the needs of the artist. Large, thick sculptures will require a clay body that shrinks less and allows for moisture to escape easily (see photo below).

Thin, uniform shapes can be made from clay bodies that shrink considerably. Generally, clay bodies shrink by between 5 and 20% from their initial wet state. Shrinking occurs at all stages: from wet to dry, during bisquing and during glaze firing. The amount of shrinkage will depend on the materials used in the clay body.

A simplified way of looking at this is to divide the materials commonly used in making clay bodies into those that reduce shrinkage and those that increase it. This is relatively easy. Clays, such as kaolins and ball clays, tend to be those materials in clay bodies that increase shrinkage, whereas the use of grogs, alumina, silica and feldspars will see shrinkage decrease.

There are two factors that cause an increasing or decreasing amount of shrinkage in materials. First, a large particle size in a given material will generally decrease the amount of shrinkage, while a fine particle size will tend to increase it. Second, some of the molecules change shape during firing. This shape change can result in either an increase or a decrease in size. Under normal circumstances, particles partially

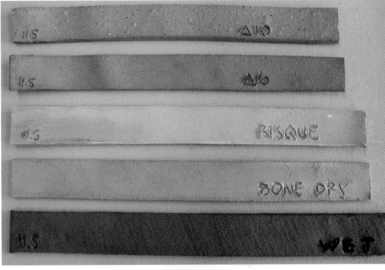

left Alan Foxley, *White Form Two*, 2008. 89 x 48 x 23cm (35 x 19 x 9in.) Coil- and slab-built. Flattened areas decorated with manganese dioxide and black copper oxide; white areas decorated with a porcelain, feldspar and gum arabic slip. Once-fired to 1280°C (2336°F) in a gas-fired reduction kiln, then fired again (same temperature) following a wash of manganese and copper. *Photo by the artist.*

top Clay strips showing shrinkage at each stage of the process: wet clay, dry clay, bisque-fired clay, and after firing to stoneware temperatures.

bottom Examples of 'home made' clays with different colourants added. *Photos by Jennifer A. Siegel.*

melt and form closer bonds with each other, thereby causing an overall size decrease. However, some less common materials, such as kyanite, actually increase in size over much of the firing range for pottery.

Colouring your clay can add to its personality and help you create the effect you want. Many colourants used for glazes can be incorporated into clays; however, coming in contact with these colourants for extended periods can be very hazardous. With regard to contact with the skin, the following table (see right) lists colourants/variegating agents that can be added safely to a clay body.

To add a colourant to a clay body, simply measure out the amount you want to add, sprinkle this on a table top, and wedge the clay on top of it until it mixes in. You can also mix two different coloured clays together, either completely to create a mid tone, or incompletely to create a marbled effect. However, adding other colourants to a clay body should generally be avoided for health and safety reasons. Adding small amounts of stains and colourants to a light-coloured clay using gloves is considered safe when creating millefiore ware, for example, but extra precautions should be taken to ensure the clay does not dry out and become airborne, as metal toxicity can result from breathing the dust of many colourants.

CLAY STORAGE

Storing your clay for a few weeks or longer before using it can have its benefits. The growth of mould in the clay, as well as the complete wetting of the materials, will usually impart a greater degree of workability to a clay body

Clays that have been delivered in their wet state have probably already aged sufficiently, but if you are making your own clay bodies from dry materials, allow the wet mixture to stand for as

Table 2: Safe-for-skin-contact colourants to add to a clay body		
Material	Colour response in clay body	% by weight used in clay body
Iron oxide	Reds, browns, blacks	0–20
Crocus martis	Similar to iron oxide, but not as pure so will provide some variegation	0–10
Titanium dioxide	Depending on mesh size, will provide white specks or general whitening	0–5
Grog (fine, medium or coarse)	Depending on the grog, will provide specking of light or dark colours	0–25
Basalt	Black specks or darkening	0–5
Illmenite	Black specks or darkening	0–5
Rutile	Contains iron and titanium, so will create light and dark variegations, sometimes yellowish/gold hues	0–10

long as possible before use. Mould in clay provides an extra level of plasticity due to its inherent sticky properties. Some people add small amounts of corn starch, flour or bread to their clay body during mixing to provide food for the mould to really get it growing!

Clay with mould on it can be a good thing! Aged and mouldy clay can often exhibit heightened plasticity.

PARTICLE SIZE, SHAPE AND PLASTICITY

The tiniest particles, which make up the bulk of a clay body, are so small that several could fit inside a single bacterium! These tiny pieces are shaped like tiny flat plates and can only be seen using a strong microscope. An average-size grain of sand would be nearly one thousand times bigger than an average particle of clay!

Different clay bodies can have very different average particle sizes, depending on the materials they are made from. These differences in average particle size have a profound effect on the way clay bodies behave. Those bodies with too small an average are waxy and sticky and have very little strength when wet. Bodies with too large an average size tend to be crumbly and not hold together, no matter how much water we add. Those clay bodies with the greatest all-round use tend to have a mixture of particles: small ones to make the bigger ones stick together; bigger ones to keep the clay from being too sticky and give it some strength

Making a clay body

Clay bodies are fairly simple to make, and the process does not require precise computations. Any difficulty lies in the actual manipulation of the materials. If you do not have a clay mixer or a pug mill, making more than a few pounds at a time will prove to be very hard work, though it can be done. There are many ways to take the work out of the process, and most of these involve mixing the ingredients in as wet a form as possible, then drying them down until they are in a more usable form, then wedging them by hand or running the clay through a pug mill.

For a stoneware body, simply start with Table 3. Look at the suggested percentages and try a mixture. As the percentages are listed by weight, you will need a scale, but you can try doing it by volume as well and see what comes of it. Clay bodies are largely very forgiving, and nothing too terribly bad is likely to happen if the mixture is not made to exacting measurements. It does make sense to do a very small amount at first and test-fire it in a bowl of previously tested clay to protect your kiln shelf in case of melting. If at first your clay melts or bloats, add more refractory (meaning heat-resistant) ingredients (the first five materials listed are more refractory). If your clay remains too open and unvitrified, add some of the materials that will lower the melting temperature (any of the last six materials listed). Substitutions can be made for the ingredients listed (see the appendices for UK and US equivalents).

To make a low-fire earthenware body, add a greater percentage of any of the last six materials in the table.

To mix your clay body, first weigh out each ingredient and put them all together in a bucket. Mix the dry ingredients together well before adding water. Do not forget to add colourants if

Table 3: Materials used in stoneware clay bodies (cone 6 to 10)	
Material	Normal percentages
Stoneware clay	40–90
Fire clay	0–30
Kaolin	0–40
Silica	0–20
Grog (usually fine)	0–20
Feldspar (potash or soda)	0–20
Ball clay	10–30
Earthenware clay (you can use your wild clay here)	0–50
Bentonite (adds plasticity)	0–5
Wollastonite	0–5
Talc	0–5

you wish (see Table 2, p.26) or some of your wild clay. If mixing a small amount, then add water bit by bit and start wedging the clay until it is well mixed. With larger amounts it is often best to add an excess of water to ensure that all the particles get completely wet, which can take several days. Use a stirring stick to work in the water, stirring it up until the clay mix is wet and mucky (forming a 'slurry' type of mixture). Then spread out the mixture and let it dry down to a usable consistency. This process can be sped up by spreading the clay on an absorbent surface, such as a plaster slab. Once it has dried to a workable consistency, wedge up the clay and give it a go!

when wet. As described earlier, particle size also influences shrinkage, so coming up with a clay body that will do all the things we need it to do can take some time. Experimenting with the basic ingredients can be an illuminating process. Try making your own clay body following the project described above.

SAFETY

One of the main hazards when working with clay is the dust produced by dry materials. Maintaining an atmosphere free of dust is important for the long-term respiratory health of all those working in the studio environment. Additionally, clay and ceramic materials are heavy! Use caution when lifting

heavy loads, and get help lifting things whenever possible. Wheeled carts and hand-trucks can be a great help in reducing these hazards. See the safety section of Chapter 3 and the appendix on studio safety and environmental health for additional safety information.

3
METHODS OF WORKING

GETTING STARTED

Most people do not start working with clay on their own without first experimenting with it in a school setting of one sort or another. If you are interested in working with clay and have never before taken a class, it is highly recommended that you get a little 'clay behind your ears', literally and figuratively, before setting off on your own.

There are many choices to make when first working with clay. Ahead of you are a myriad of possible paths: types of clay, ways of making things, ways of firing things, different glazes and decorating methods, and so on and so on. Many choices are dictated by available resources, space, money and time. Most experienced clay artists would recommend that you start off small and work toward your own methods and habits, purchasing additional equipment and tools as needed. By proceeding cautiously like this, you will avoid wasting resources.

Most people associate clay work with a potter's wheel, a kiln and a clay studio. Often there are glazes and lots of hand tools, and sometimes bigger electric machines for manipulating the clay. There is a funny thing about clay and the people who work with it: some people recognise straightaway that they are working with mud – a crude, common, dirty, messy and often free material. Other people see clay as a highly technical material that can be shaped and hardened with computer-assisted machines.

For the first group, the clay is often shaped by hand, work is done outside, and the clean-up is left to natural processes. Clay sculptures are sometimes 'finished' when they are dry, and firing the work is not always necessary (however, sculptors working in this way are few and far between). People in the second group tend to think in terms of the chemical makeup of clay and have books about

A group of students discussing glazes suitable for their clay. *Photos by Jennifer A. Siegel.*

physics in their studios; their kilns are controlled by computers, and the periodic table of elements is on the wall of the glazing area. Some of those in this group manage to leave the studio at the end of the day cleaner than when they arrived. People's personalities tend to dictate what sort or relationship develops between them and clay; and luckily, clay is well suited to both mud-wrestlers and neat-freaks. The vast majority of people that work with clay, whether by sculpting, handbuilding, or throwing, fall in between these extremes. Very few artists refrain from firing their finished pieces, and very few as well think in terms of the atomic structure of their dishware.

No one can master all the different techniques, and most people would not want to try. It is, however, advantageous early on to become aware of as many different techniques as possible, and to begin to make decisions as to which method of working most appeals to you. Once you have identified a direction that suits you, develop as deep an understanding of the techniques involved as

possible. Some people remain clay students for life, taking new classes each year and trying out new techniques. This habit can be endlessly rewarding, but if your goal is to become proficient and marketable, then focusing on a few techniques over many years usually proves to be the most rewarding approach.

Choosing your clay body

The first choice to make when working with clay is to choose the clay body you will work with. A clay body is composed of several different kinds of raw clay, plus other ingredients to make it look and feel a certain way (see p.20). Your chosen clay body will need to be able to withstand your methods of working (e.g. not be too hard or too soft), look good to you when fired, and fire to the correct cone. (For now, 'cone' can be thought of as interchangeable with 'temperature'. Cones and temperature will be discussed more fully in Chapter 4).

If your goal is to handbuild – which means making things away from the potter's wheel – then you will often need a clay body with a somewhat grittier feel, especially if you are planning to build bigger and thicker pieces. Wheel-throwers frequently find that smoother clays are easier on their hands, especially when first learning to centre. Most existing studios will have clays designated for the wheel or for handbuilding, and most manufacturers can recommend clay bodies that will have the right 'feel' for your purpose. As discussed in Chapter 2, the particle size in the clay you choose will dictate both the way the clay feels and how much it will shrink. Wheel-throwers can normally get away with using smoother clay bodies with smaller particles and a higher shrinkage; handbuilders using the same clay bodies run the risk of cracks developing in the work.

The colour of the clay really comes down to personal choice. Most teaching studios will only have a few choices in this regard. You will probably be glazing your pieces later, so the colour might not really matter that much as the clay will mostly be covered anyway. However, the colour response of the glazes over light-coloured clay bodies will be quite different than over dark ones. If you are looking for bright glaze colours, choose a light-coloured clay body; if you desire more muted tones, go for a darker one.

In an existing studio the firing temperatures of the kilns and the maturing temperatures of the clays in use will have been coordinated. Most manufacturers and studios describe their pre-mixed wet clays in general terms by the cone (again, think temperature for now) at which they mature.

So, which clay to choose? If you are new to making things with clay, especially if you are planning to use the wheel, choose an inexpensive clay because there is a lot of wastage at the

Penelope Withers, *Two Freeform Bottles*, 2007, ht: 50 and 51cm (19½ and 20in.). Fired to 1280°C (2336°F) in an electric kiln. *Photo by Ken Fisher.*

start. Many teaching facilities will have a clay recycling programme that you can take advantage of. If not, start one! (see p.64 for advice on recycling). Frequently there will be free clay for you to use if you are willing to help with the recycling process. If attending a class, take the teacher's advice as they will have a good idea as to what clay will best suit your experience level and goals. If you are working on your own your choice will be harder. The most important aspect will be to make sure the clay you choose will not melt at the cone you plan to fire to. So, what cone should you fire to? Read on!

Firing temperatures and cones

People fire clay to many different temperatures, with a huge variety of results. Very low firing temperatures, which for clay means anything below about 350°C (662°F), will have no effect on the clay other than to make it hot. Above 350°C (662°F), the chemically bound water (see Chapter 2) will start to be driven off. Once this process has been completed, the clay will no longer be affected by becoming wet, meaning it is no longer clay but is now a ceramic material that will not disintegrate in water. Most people firing pots in modern kilns think about firing their pots somewhere in the range between 900°C (1652°F) and 1300°C (2372°F). Low-fire (earthenware) clays tend to mature – but not melt – in the range between 900 and 1050°C (1652 and 1922°F); mid-range clays mature from about 1050 to 1200°C (1922 to 2192°F); and high-fire clays (including porcelain) mature between 1200 and 1300°C (2192 and 2372°F) – see also pp.21–3 for photos of fired clays. Some considerations to bear in mind when choosing what temperature you will fire to:

Victoria Christen, *Pink Watering Pot*, 2005, 15 x 7.5 x 12.5cm (6 x 3 x 5in). Red earthenware with coloured clay slips, thrown and altered, fired to cone 04. *Photo by Courtney Frisse.*

• How high can your kiln fire? Some kilns are not powerful enough to fire above a certain temperature.

• How long do you want your firings to last? Higher temperatures generally take longer to reach.

• How about cost? It is more expensive to heat kilns to higher temperatures.

However, many low-temperature glazes are more expensive than high-temperature glazes, partially offsetting the increase in firing cost.

• What sort of effects do you want to achieve? This last consideration is a complicated area and therefore hard to summarise succinctly. Very generally, after firing, high-fire pottery tends to feel more durable and look a bit more like stone (hence the common name 'stoneware'), but an awful lot of the same effects can be achieved at lower temperatures as well. Low-fire or earthenware clay is usually porous (after firing) and can feel like the terracotta clay used to make traditional flowerpots. High-fire glazes tend to have more subdued colours with a narrower palate of colours to choose from, while lower-temperature glazes and decorations are often brighter and utilise many different colours.

To keep things simple, for now we will focus on the three most common cones people fire to: 04, 6 and 10 (see p.70–71 and the cone table on p.154). Those who fire to earthenware temperatures often fire to cone 04, or about 1050°C (1922°F). Those who fire to mid-range temperatures usually fire to cone 6, or about 1180°C (2156°F), and those that fire to high-fire temperatures usually fire to cone 10, or about 1260°C (2300°F). You will tend to find a lot of information available for these particular cones, especially with regard to glaze recipes, and far less for other cones.

For those just setting out, one way to get started initially is simply to find a piece of finished pottery that you like, then try and determine what cone it was fired to. Make that your starting point. If you have seen some stoneware bowls that excite you made from buff-coloured clay, then purchase some high-fire buff stoneware clay (and make sure you can fire to sufficiently high temperatures in the kiln you will be using). If you are drawn to some brightly coloured tiles that are made from earthenware clay, purchase some low-fire clay. It is best, of course, to go into the making process with the right materials, so spending a little time at first thinking about what it is you hope to achieve and acquiring the materials that will allow you to do this will be time well spent.

CLAY TOOLS: HAND TOOLS

Clearly, the tools you will need will depend on how you will be working with the clay. Sculptors and handbuilders will need a different array of tools than people working on the wheel. Some artists prefer to make their own tools, which helps to personalise their work. If you want your pieces to be as individual as possible, then starting with handmade tools is an important first step.

It is faster to just buy readymade tools, but consider at least making a few tools yourself; they can be as simple as a whittled stick or a shaped piece of plastic (such as a cut-up old credit card).

Here are some recommendations for tools needed for working with clay in specific ways, listed in order of how commonly they are used.

Having access to woodworking machines can allow you to make a wide variety of your own clay tools.

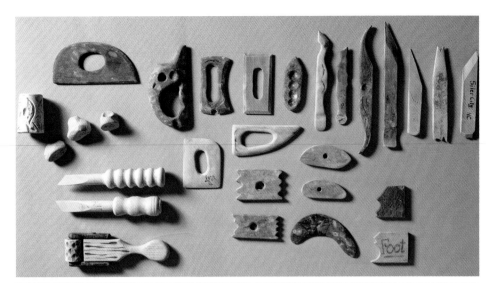

Throwing

Essentials
Sponge
Needle tool/pin tool
Wooden knife*
Wooden ribs*
Wire-cutting tool*
Rubber/plastic ribs (old CDs and cut-up credit cards work well)*
Loop tools for trimming/turning*
Paintbrush*
Old towel/cloth
Water bucket/container

Useful items
Wooden bats*
Callipers*
Bisqued trimming chucks*
Foot (the base of a pot) shaping wood profile tool*
Metal fluting tools*
Metal scraper
Wood profile tools*
Rim-shaping wood tool*
Wooden jigs (for mugs, bowls, vases, crocks or canisters)*
Wooden paddle*
Wooden pot lifters or cradles*
Wooden throwing stick*

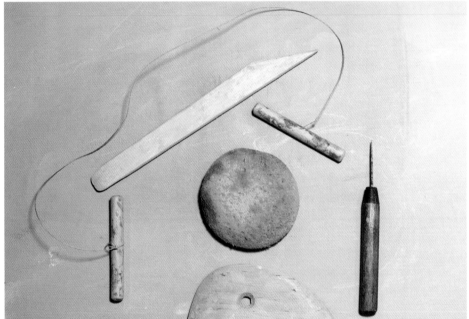

Handbuilding/Sculpting

Ruler/straight edge
Canvas-covered work boards*
Fettling knife
Loop tools *
Modelling wood tools*
Rolling pin*
Rubber ribs
Sponge
Wire-cutting tool*
Wooden ribs*
Hand extruder
Plaster slump or hump moulds*
Sculpting stands/broadwheel
Wooden paddle*
Spray bottle (to keep work damp)

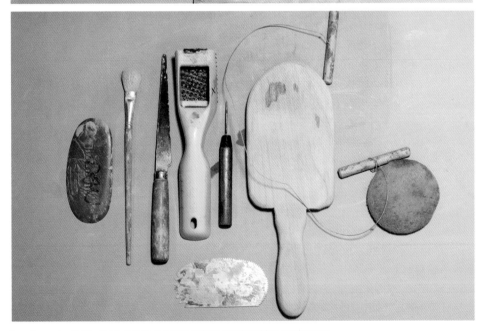

An * next to a tool indicates those that can be made at home using simple tools.

top An array of clay tools made at home using woodworking equipment.
middle Tools used when throwing on the wheel.
above Some tools used for handbuilding.

May Criado, *Disco,* 2007, 42 x 11 x 45cm (16½ x 4¼ x 17¾ in.). Stoneware and porcelain assembled slabs. Fired to 1250°C (2282°F). *Photo by Xose Abad.*

Tilemaking

Ruler/straight edge
Canvas-covered work boards*
Rolling pin*
Rubber ribs
Sponge
Wooden modelling tools*
Wooden ribs*
Miniature rolling pins with
 imprinting designs*
Press moulds, plaster*
Slip-trail bottle
Tile cutters

An * next to a tool indicates those that can be most easily made at home using simple tools.

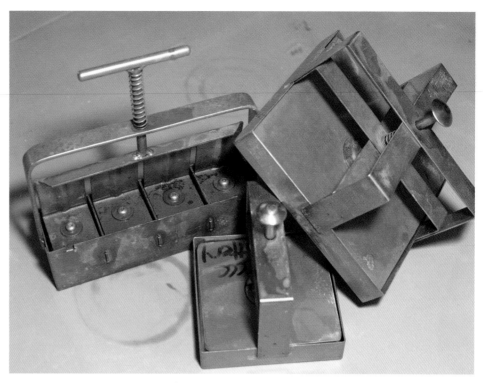

Speciality tile cutters for those making lots of clay tiles of a specific shape.

STUDIO SET-UP AND EQUIPMENT

Setting up a complete studio is a big job no matter how you look at it. Having a large dedicated space in which to make things with clay is optimal in one sense in that the mess created by the clay is kept away from other activities, but making things from clay in small multipurpose spaces is common practice. Simply sitting out in the garden or at the kitchen counter with a board and some clay can be space enough for many projects. Finding a space for a wheel and kiln can be a bit trickier. Small wheels are made now that can fit in closets and under counters, and small kilns can be located outside next to a garage or patio under a metal shed roof if need be. Pottery can be and always has been created in the most primitive of situations, so don't be put off if you don't have a room to dedicate to your craft. Remember, however, that many of the chemicals used in making

ceramics are hazardous: keep them away from food and food preparation areas and out of reach of children. Be sure also to wipe surfaces down afterwards to eliminate clay dust.

Most people working with clay have as a minimum the following requirements for a 'studio' set-up:

A table to work on
Access to water
Some hand tools
Shelves for storing work/materials
Buckets for storing materials/scrap
 clay/glazes
A kiln or access to a kiln/firing method
A scale for weighing clay/glaze
 ingredients
A sieve for glazes
People choosing to make round pots will
 often need a wheel, but round pots can

also be made by coiling. In addition, it is convenient to have a small sturdy table specifically for wedging your clay – one that is made of plaster and can therefore also be used to dry out very wet clay is extremely handy. Wedging tables often have a wire strung over them for quick cutting to assist the wedging/de-airing process. More information on wedging can be found later in this chapter.

Other pieces of equipment that can be purchased and used but are by no means essential for making things with clay are:

A pug mill
A wall-mounted extruder
A clay mixer
A spray booth
A slab roller

The de-airing pugmill is used to blend soft clays together and remove trapped air bubbles, effectively wedging the clay for you. The output end of the machine can also be used as a horizontal power extruder.

left A wall-mounted extruder can be used to quickly make a variety of shapes, much like a larger version of a child's play-dough machine.

above A clay mixer is not normally found in a home studio — they lend themselves to larger facilities for mixing or recycling large amounts of clay on a regular basis.

THROWING

Once you have chosen your clay body, perhaps purchased some equipment and found a place to set it up, it is time to start making things! Truly, the best way to learn to make pieces on the wheel is to take a class and have a teacher with experience show you how to position your hands and body with the equipment you are using so as to give you the best chance of success.

If this is your first go at attempting work on the wheel, then the following motto should never be far from your mind: Give yourself the chance to be a beginner!

People often give up making pottery only because they expect 'good' results too soon. Be patient and give yourself time to develop your skills.

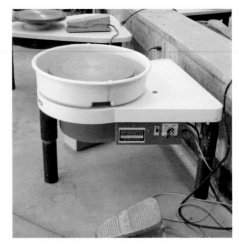

above Electric wheels come in many shapes and sizes. Find one that works for you ergonomically and fits in the space available to you. *Photo by Jennifer A. Siegel.*
below A kick wheel. *Photo by Noah Riedel.*

top A spray booth takes up a lot of space, but allows artists to apply glazes to awkward and heavy pieces. *Photo by Jennifer A. Siegel.*
above A slab roller is nice if working extensively with large slabs, but often a rolling pin will do the job more quickly. *Photo by Cathy Kiffney.*

These larger pieces of equipment tend to be cost-prohibitive for most people and are generally unnecessary for people beginning with clay. As you develop your skills and style, purchasing a larger piece of equipment will be of great help in producing work on a larger scale.

Mark Hewitt, *Teapot*, 2007, ht: 12.5cm (5 in.). Thrown and assembled teapot, wood-fired and salt-glazed. *Photo by Jason Dowdle.*

Learning to make pieces: Centring, opening and pulling up the walls

For most people it is not how much time they spend on the wheel practising throwing that will have the biggest impact on their skill development (although without regular practice the basic skills will never be learned). More important than the total time spent at the wheel is the number of times you 'start over' with centring and, as an offshoot of that, how much clay you have attempted to centre.

Most people can usually centre 0.5–1kg (1–2lbs) of clay reliably and easily after having attempted a total of about 450kg (1000lbs), 1–2lbs at a time. Although this may sound like a lot, each attempt will only require a few minutes – usually before something goes wrong! Spending lots of time on the wheel practising the wrong thing, i.e. practising attempting to save a piece that has gone 'wrong', is not time well spent! A hundred hours spent learning how to centre and develop a simple form properly will require starting over about every 5 minutes, at the end of which you will indeed have practised with more than 450kg (1000lbs) of clay. A hundred hours spent trying to save failing pieces will not teach you what you need to learn, and you will also spend far more than 5 minutes on each attempt.

Opening up the clay to create a base for a pot.

Pulling up the walls of a vessel.

Here are 20 steps for throwing an upright shape on the wheel (flat, plate-like shapes will be discussed in the next section).

For beginners, your very first project is to just centre the clay and not worry about whether or not it turns into anything. Centring clay is a process of evenly distributing the clay you are using in the middle of the wheel, so that it looks nice and round and smooth, sits centrally on the wheelhead in a contained lump, and doesn't wobble when the wheel is turning.

Step 1. First, accurately weigh out the correct amount of clay for what you plan to make **(1)**.

Experienced potters will know about how much clay to use for their project. For beginners, the very best thing you can do to make your life easier when first working on the wheel is to simply start with the same small amount of clay each time. Be sure to have a scale for weighing clay, and measure out several 0.7 kg (1.5lb) balls of clay at the beginning of each session. Using the same amount of clay each time will give you the chance to practise the same moves in the same way each time, and this will allow for the most rapid development of your skills.

Step 2. Wedge your clay into a ball **(2B)** (more information about wedging clay can be found later in this chapter) and plop it (this is where the term 'throwing' comes from, but it's really more of a 'plop' or a slap) down onto the centre of a wheelhead that is dry and clean, assuming it's your first piece of the day **(2A)**. If you've already been working, then plop it onto the thin clay circle left behind by your previous piece/attempt after you cut if off with a wire tool. Patting it into a rough cone shape first can also help the process **(2C)**.

A common problem at first is that the clay refuses to stick and keeps coming off the wheel. This can be very frustrating. If any water gets between your clay

Weighing the clay on a scale prior to throwing.

Once your clay is prepared, slap the ball of prepared clay onto the wheelhead as near the centre as you can.

and the wheelhead, the clay will come off when you push on it to get it centred. If this happens, remove the clay and dry the wheel with a towel, then dry your clay and start again. Each time you cut a piece off the wheel with the wire tool, leave the remaining clay, a thin circle, on the wheel and place your next piece on this circle; it will stick well.

Step 3. Squish down the edges of the clay to seal it to the wheelhead **(3)** . It's not much of a technical term, but squishing the clay is an important step. Press the edges down to the wheelhead to keep water from getting underneath.

Step 4. Use your sponge with the wheel turning to further seal the clay to the wheelhead **(4)**.

Step 5. Finally, it is time to add water! Water is both your friend and your enemy when throwing. It keeps the clay slippery, but over time it also weakens the clay. As a beginner, do not worry about how much water you are using. Keep your hands wet and keep the clay wet and slick – this will help with centring. As you improve, centring will take less time and ultimately you will use much less water **(5)**.

Step 6. Keeping your hands together, with the wheel spinning anticlockwise, push down your 0.7kg (1.5lb) ball or cone of clay until it is about 5cm (2in.) thick. Apply more water when it loses its slipperiness.

Look at the images and practise holding your hands as shown. It is very important that you keep your hands together. Do not push the clay down too far or you will not be able to push it back up again. If it does get flattened, just use your wire to remove it and start again **(6)**.

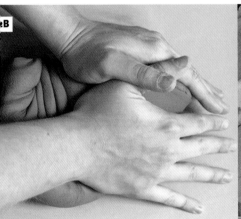
Wedging clay in preparation for throwing.

Plopping the clay on the wheel firmly helps to get it to stick.

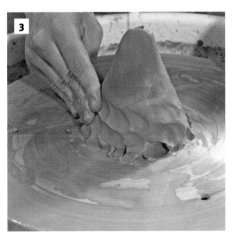
Squish around the edges of the clay before applying water to help get it to stick.

Use your sponge to completely seal edge of clay to wheel before adding water.

With wet hands, begin by pushing down on the top of the clay. This begins the centring process and helps further attach the clay to the wheel.

An example of clay that has been pushed down too far. If this happens, it's best to remove it and start again.

Step 7. Keeping your hands together, push the clay from the side until it 'cones' (not to be confused with the term 'cone' that has to do with the firing temperature in a kiln! In this case, it's just referring to the shape of the clay) back up and is about 10cm (4in.) tall (if you are using 1.5lb/0.7kg of clay) **(7A)**. Apply more water when it loses its slipperiness. If you are sitting at an electric wheel, be sure to rest your left elbow on your left knee when you do this move **(7B)**. Use props under your foot if you need to raise your elbow. If standing or using a kick wheel, brace your left arm against your side as best as you can. The clay will want to push you around, but be as firm and as steady as possible.

Step 8. Repeat steps 5 and 7 until the clay is centred (which is easier said than done!) Your last move should be the downward motion (see image 9), before you move on to opening up the clay (step 10). Getting your clay centred consistently will take many, many attempts. Sometimes, the clay might just come off in your hands or fly off the wheel. This is perfectly OK and is bound to happen. Just use your wire to remove the rest of the clay from the wheel, remove the clay slime from your hands using the edge of your scrap bucket, then get a new ball of clay and start again. Starting again is important! Start again often, and don't waste your time attempting to fix a lump of clay that has become too wobbly.

Above all, remember to have fun and don't be worried if things don't go to plan. Again, the best thing you can do to learn how to centre is to repeatedly start over, practising the initial moves until you get them right. If the clay gets too crazy or floppy, drop it in the recycling bucket and get a new piece (what to do with that bucket full of scraps will be discussed later under Clay recycling, see p.64).

7A After pushing the clay down, use your hands together to cone the clay back up again.

7B Good body position can make all the difference when centring. Be sure to keep your left elbow on your leg (alternatively, you can use the splash guard if your wheel has one). Boosting your foot up on blocks can help.

If your clay gets just too far off centre to continue, then it's time to start again!

Opening the clay using thumbs.

Step 9. Deciding when the clay is centred enough to continue can be tricky **(9)**. Perfectly centring a piece of clay is physically impossible – it will never be absolutely perfect. On the other hand, as the wheel is spinning, if there is a noticeable wobble then you should continue trying to centre it. If while the wheel is turning you don't feel the clay pushing you back and forth when you apply light pressure, then it is probably good enough. If you are unsure, try holding the clay with both hands and shutting your eyes – you will soon feel any wobbles. You have to be somewhat forgiving at first, but equally you won't be able to develop an even, round form if you are overly forgiving. After centring the clay, follow the next steps.

An example of well-centred clay ready to open up.

Opening the clay using the index finger.

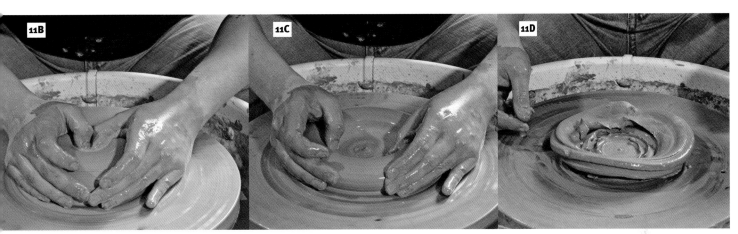

Opening the clay using thumbs.

Opening the clay further with thumbs.

If you pull outwards too far at this stage, the top ring of clay will come off the base. Time to start over.

Step 10. Once centred, the next thing to do is open up the clay. Before proceeding, make sure your clay has a flattened top. Keeping your hands together and keeping your arms well braced use your index finger or middle finger very slowly and carefully to push down just to the right of dead centre on your clay **(10)**.

With the wheel turning, push slowly downward until you are about 1cm (½in.) from the wheelhead. Measure this using your needle tool: push the needle tool through the clay near the middle, slide a fingertip down the side of the needle to the top of the clay, and pull the needle tool out. The distance from your fingertip to the tip of the needle tool will give you

a good idea of how much clay is there. If it is too thick, keep going as before and measure again; if too thin, you can push a little ball of clay down into the hole and blend it in with a sponge.

Step 11. Widen the hole you have made by pulling the clay towards you while the wheel is turning using two fingers. Keep your hands together and brace your arms on your body. Alternatively, you can use your thumbs to pull out to the sides. Either way, do not pull too far and ensure you pull slowly and evenly **(11A–C)**.

This is often where a doughnut-shaped ring of clay accidently comes off **(11D)**. To avoid this, stop opening

the hole before the fledgling clay wall that is forming begins to lean outwards.

Step 12. With the wheel turning, gently smooth everything out with your sponge and remove any standing water in the centre. This is a good time to compact the clay in the bottom centre of your piece. Use a sponge or rib to push down lightly in the centre, and work from the centre out and then back in. This will help to prevent the dreaded 'S' crack that can form in the bottom of pieces as they dry. Before proceeding, make sure the short walls that you now have are the same thickness from top to bottom. If not, smooth them with a sponge until they are. Pulling up uneven walls is very, very tricky, and not a skill you should have to develop.

Step 13. Preparing to pull up the walls. This step is the most dramatic and fun to watch, but its success is predicated on all the proceeding steps having gone according to plan. Pulling up the walls is not very hard if you start with an even, well-centred piece. Again, starting over when things go wrong will help you get better at the early steps, which are fundamental to making a successful piece. Before you begin to pull the walls up, even out any bumps in the thick ring of clay at the bottom. Try to make sure it is an even thickness all round **(13A and 13B)**.

To pull up the walls, follow these steps:

Step 14. First moisten the clay with your sponge, but try not to fill up the middle with water. Make your two hands into a claw shape **(14)**. Keep hands together and keep your elbows braced on your torso throughout the move.

top Before continuing to develop the shape, smooth out any uneven parts of the low stumpy walls. This will make pulling them upwards a great deal easier.
above Smoothed and ready to go.

Lyn Morrow, *Covered Jar*, 2008, 46 x 28cm (18 x 11in.). Copper microcrystalline glaze on porcelain, fired to cone 11. From the collection of Bruce Foster. *Photo by Catherine Whitten.*

Step 15. With the wheel spinning, using your index fingers, push into the walls on the inside and outside of the piece – your right hand will be on the outside of the piece and your left hand will be on the inside with the clay moving away from you (wheel spinning anticlockwise). Try to keep your other fingers out of the way **(15A and 15B)**.

Step 16. With the wheel still spinning at a medium speed, slowly and carefully draw your hands and fingers upwards. The relationship between wheel speed and hand movement is critical, and hard to get exactly right at first. Also difficult to get right is the amount of pressure to apply with your fingers. There should be enough pressure exerted through the clay between your right index finger on the outside and your left index finger on the inside to produce a thinner, taller wall when you pull upwards. Your upward pull should also be slow enough that all points of the clay wall are touched by your fingers as you move upwards. In other words, there should

be a continuous spiral up the sides (inside and outside). When the pull is complete, there should be a series of little lines up the side that are very close together **(16A)**. As you improve, these lines will become more spread out.

If you find that, after you have pulled up, the walls have not become at least a little taller, you need to apply more pressure. Alternatively, if you have gone through the wall and a clay ring has come off in your hands, then you need to back off a bit on the pressure with your next piece of clay **(16B)**.

This is a good hand position when learning to pull up the walls of a pot. Keeping your hands together will minimize wobbles.

Here is how it should look as you apply pressure at the base of the walls and begin to pull up.

Pulling the walls up. You can see the bulk of the clay as a ring being pulled to the top.

The lines on the sides of your clay after each pull can give you a visual description of the relationship between the speed of your wheel and the speed of your hand movements.

When pulling up, if you squeeze the clay too hard, it will wobble and tear. Time to start again.

Step 17. Repeat Step 16 several times until the wall is tall enough and thin enough. Before each pull, drip some water on the top of the wall so that it runs down both the inside and the outside. Each time you pull up, your cylinder should get a bit taller. Raising the cylinder by 1.5cm (1in.) each pull means things are going well: you are applying the right amount of pressure and maximising your progress. Many people aim to be able to pull the clay up until it is very thin **(17)**, but the thinner the clay is the more likely the pot is to collapse, so you may want to start off with thicker walls until you improve. Other people like to keep things a bit thicker, even after their skills develop,

for any number of good reasons – for instance, they like the way a good sturdy piece feels.

Step 18. Making a finished shape out of a cylinder is the final step in making pieces on the wheel. Nearly all shapes except flat, plate-like shapes can be made from cylinders **(18A)**.

To make a bowl, pull up a cylinder that is quite thick, and then use a hand on the inside (often with the help of a sponge or rib) to spread the cylinder outwards **(18B, 18C, 18D and 18E)**.

To make a curved pot, throw a taller cylinder and push the middle part outwards from the inside; it can help to

leave a bit of extra clay in the parts of the cylinder you plan to push out **(19)**. It is also possible to 'collar' the neck on some pots to make a more dramatic shape **(19A, 19B and 19C)**.

Play around with these techniques and see what assortment of shapes you can come up with.

Keep an eye on how high you can pull your cylinders, how straight and narrow you can keep them, and how much time it takes for you to complete them from the time you first add water to the time you finish your last upward pull. You will find with practice that the amount of time required will decrease dramatically, and this will also greatly improve the

A nice straight cylinder made from about 1kg (2.2lb) of clay.

A short cylinder ready to be made into a bowl.

Beginning to shape a cylinder into a bowl using a rib. C of the curved sides of the rib is held against the inside w

Carefully applying pressure to the inside of a cylinder to form a belly. Help can be given by the other hand supporting the wall on the outside.

Collaring a cylinder to make the form narrower.

quality of the finished work for one simple reason: the faster you work, the less time the clay has to absorb water and become floppy. You might think that starting with dryer clay would be a good idea – and it is, to a point – but dry clay is very hard to centre. Wet clay is somewhat easier to centre, but hard to make stand up in any shape. You have to find a happy medium, and take advantage of the clay's softness and strength at different points in the development of your piece.

right Noah Riedel, small mug, 2008, 7.5 x 10 x 10cm (3 x 4 x 4in). Stoneware, chun glaze, once-fired to cone 7 in oxidation. *Photo by Seth Tice-Lewis.*

18C

Continuing to shape a cylinder into a bowl using a rib.

18D

The bowl after shaping with the rib.

18E

A cut-through of the bowl shows even walls, and enough clay at the base to trim a foot later.

19B

As collaring progresses the neck gets gradually more narrow.

19C

Smoothing out the top rim having collared in the neck.

Throwing a plate

Step 1. To make a plate, first attach a bat to the wheelhead (see p.51). Follow the steps for centring, but do not open up the middle with your index finger (Step 10 on p.43). Instead, after centring, continue to push down on the centred circle of clay until it is good and flat, and about 2cm (1in.) thick **(1)**. Using a wooden bat under your plate will enable you to remove it later. It is very hard to get a plate off the wheel while wet without destroying it otherwise. A dinner plate requires about 3–4lb (1.4–1.8kg) of clay.

Step 2. Then, use the lower corner of the palm of your right hand (the 'corner' opposite your thumb) to depress the middle of the clay, and then push the clay outwards and away from you **(2)**. Your base should be (when finished) about 1cm (about ³⁄₈in.) thick, unless you plan to turn a foot on it later, in which case you should leave it about 1.5cm/⅝in. thick.

Step 3. Use your left hand on its side against the wheelhead to support your right hand as it moves outwards. Stop pushing before you reach the edge, and then work the edge up and outwards into the rim of your plate **(3A & 3B)**. If you tend to throw thick, heavy plates then plan on doing some trimming once it has dried to leatherhard. Image **3c** shows a thick plate in need of trimming.

When getting ready to make a plate, push the clay down further than you normally would for making upright, hollow forms.

Use your palm to push the clay outwards when making a plate. Be sure to check the thickness with a needle tool as you progress.

Once the clay is pushed outwards, begin to create the rim of the plate using your fingers to pull up a short wall.

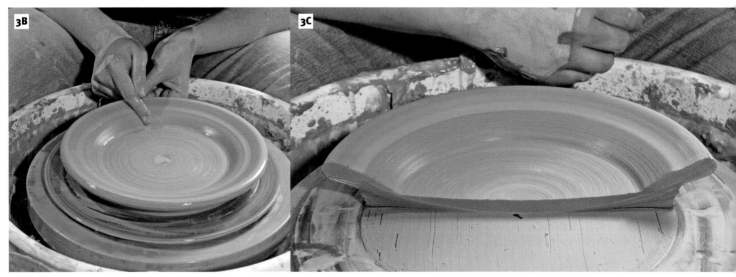

Using your fingers to support the wall underneath, gently fold it down a little, and finish off the edge of the rim.

A cut through of the finished plate, showing the thickness and profile. There is still enough clay at the edges of the base to be trimmed back a little.

Lara O'Keefe, *Crow Platter*, 2009, w: 46cm (18in.). Wood-fired and salt-glazed. *Photo by Jason Dowdle.*

Using a wire tool to cut a piece off the wheelhead, with thumbs stretching the wire taut and flat to the surface of the wheel.

When removing a piece from the wheel, hold the board exactly level with the wheelhead.

Some pieces can be picked up directly from the wheel.

Taking a finished piece off the wheel

Removing your piece from the wheel can prove to be a big challenge. There are a few tried and true methods to use. Try each one and see what works best for you.

The first method works well for small pieces that are less than about 1.8kg (4lb) with narrow bases under 12–15cm (5–6in.). First, with the wheel turning very slowly, cut under the piece with your wire tool (hold it low and tight to the wheel or it will remove the bottom of your piece!) **(1)**.

Then, turn off the wheel, put some water on the wheelhead next to the piece, and pass your wire tool through the water and under your piece several times. It often happens that once the water is under the piece completely, the piece will begin to slide around, so quickly get a board and wet it to allow the piece to slide over it. Then, holding the board level with the wheelhead with one hand, with the other hand push the piece off the wheel and onto the board in one smooth motion **(2)**.

A second method is to cut your piece off the wheel with the wire, then simply pick up the piece with your hands directly from the wheel, and place it on a ware board. This works best if you tend to throw quickly with firm clay, and you have not thrown the piece as absolutely thin as possible. Pull a wire under the piece as described above, then using the index and middle fingers of each hand near the bottom, gently lift up and move it **(3)**.

A third method involves using wooden pot lifters or cradles or even thin, flexible strips of bamboo. The idea here is to have a variety of pieces of wood with

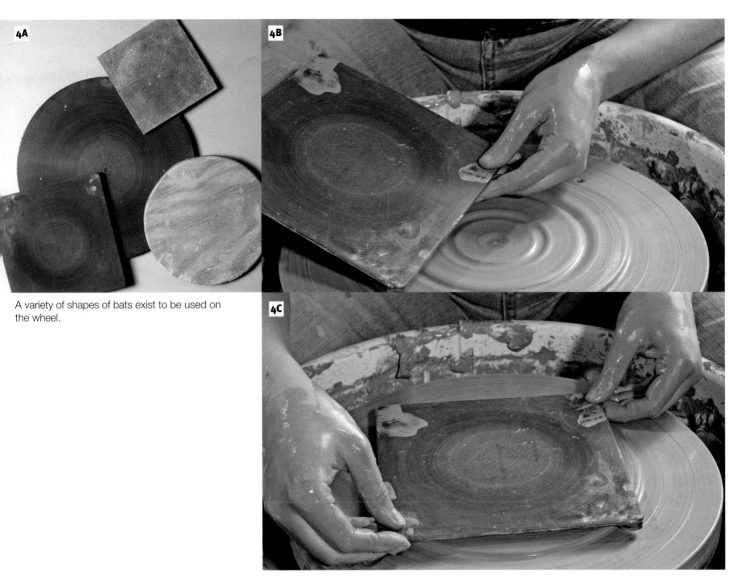

4A

4B

4C

A variety of shapes of bats exist to be used on the wheel.

Bats are best held down to the wheel using some centred, flattened clay.

pre-sized bevelled semicircles cut out of them. These press up against the sides of the base of the pot, and you simply lift and move. They tend to do some amount of 'damage' to the sides of the pot near the base, but this also tends to be easy to fix. With the flexible bamboo strips you pull each one halfway round the base, hold the ends together firmly to tighten the strips around the base, then lift and move. This one is tricky with taller pieces, but it does work!

A fourth method can be used with any size of piece, large or small, but is most often used with large, heavy pieces, or big flat pieces such as plates. This method involves putting a board, known as a 'bat', on top of the wheelhead before you begin. You can make these yourself or buy them. Some wheels have holes drilled in them for 'bat pins' (which hold the bat in place on wheels with corresponding pins on their wheelheads), if not, you can simply stick the bat down using clay. Once you have made a piece,

you pull a wire under it as usual to assist with its later release from the bat, and then remove the bat with the piece still on top of it. Quick and easy, this method does require you to have enough bats to hold all the pieces you want to make until they are dry enough to remove (**4A, 4B and 4C**).

Turning, trimming and finishing on the wheel

Most beginners find that turning or trimming a thrown piece is fun and exciting, while those that are attempting to make a living by throwing pots often try to avoid trimming as much as possible. Trimming is fun for nearly everyone at first, but it also takes time and creates a lot of clay to be recycled, and neither of these aspects results in much money being made.

In order to trim a piece, you must first allow it to dry sufficiently so that it can be turned upside down on the wheel without this causing damage to the piece. This usually happens overnight, but can take more than a day or two if the piece is large or is stored in a cool, damp atmosphere. If you need to, you can put a plastic bag or a piece of cloth over the piece to extend the drying time until you are ready to work in the studio again. However, if the piece has dried out a little too much, you can spray it with water to dampen it down again (any empty plastic bottle with a spray nozzle will do).

After drying, the piece must be centred upside down on the wheel. The simplest way for most people to centre a piece before trimming or turning is to place the pot upside down on the wheel as near to 'centred' as possible, then with the wheel turning slowly, hold your finger in a fixed position close to the inverted base or belly of the pot. While the pot slowly turns, you will be able to feel the surface brush your fingertip. If there is a point where the surface makes full contact with your finger then you need to stop the wheel and just barely nudge the pot into the centre very lightly, then continue. After several nudges, the base or belly should brush your fingertips all the way round – it's now centred! Then the piece can be fastened down with clay around the edges (1).

Once the piece is secured on the wheel, trimming commences. To start

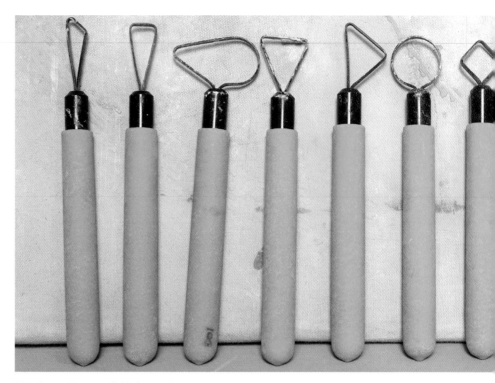
Trimming tools are available in a variety of shapes.

with, it is important to think about what your goals are for trimming. Usually, people are looking to 'improve' the shape of their piece and remove some

extra weight in the process. Others might be attempting to add a foot that will allow them to keep hold of their piece by the base when dunking it in a

Once centred, pieces must be firmly attached to the wheelhead with soft clay before trimming.

Trimming the inside of the footring.

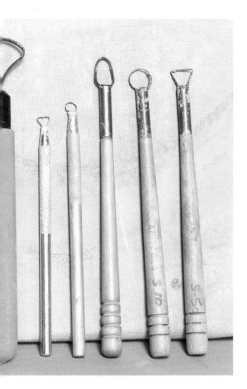

glaze! Whatever it is you are trying to do, before you turn your piece over on the wheel, take a good look at the inside and outside and make a mental note as to how much clay can be removed without making a hole. Also, while

trimming, do not spin the wheel too quickly, or the piece is likely to fly off and become another lump of clay in the recycling bucket. Using your loop tools or trim tools, remove clay around the base of the piece in ribbons **(2 and 3)**.

Applying pressure at different angles will remove either more or less clay for each revolution. Practise with different tools and see what happens. Everyone sooner or later makes a hole in the bottom or simply removes the bottom altogether. If this happens, it's best to shrug your shoulders, take a deep breath and start again! It is possible to apply a patch to the piece, but again it is in your long-term best interest to learn how to do things correctly rather than spending time learning how to fix things when they go wrong.

To finish your piece, you can smooth out the trimmed areas with a damp sponge or rib, and then sign your name on the bottom with the date and place you made it, if you want. Having a bit of history on the bottom of each piece will certainly be fun later when you compare pieces made

from different times in the past **(4 and 5)**.

Finally, leave your piece to dry. Depending on the circumstances most pieces will dry out completely in a few days, and are then ready for bisque firing. If you have applied additional features to your piece, such as handles, knobs or spouts, then it is advisable to slow down the drying process somewhat to avoid cracking. Use plastic bags or cloths to assist you in this. If you are single firing, you will want to apply a glaze to the piece before it dries out completely.

Finishing a piece off the wheel is also a good option; not all pieces need to be trimmed as described. As your skills grow, less and less clay should be left at the bottom of your pieces. You may find that careful use of your wooden ribs or wooden knife allows you to bypass trimming altogether. Some pieces may only need a quick rub of sandpaper once dry.

Trimming the outside edge.

Smoothing the bottom of a trimmed pot with a rib makes for a more finished look.

When complete, many people sign the bottom of their pots; others use a stamp with their initials or symbol on it.

Adding to your thrown work: Making handles

Handles can be made in a variety of ways. The most traditional approach is to pull a handle off the side of a leatherhard piece. To do this you must first score the side of the pot where the handle will be attached using a needle tool or an old fork. Next, roughly fashion a piece of clay for the handle and, after applying slip or water with a brush, score the end of it and press it onto the scored part of your piece. Now, wetting your hand and the handle, begin to elongate and slowly pull the handle into shape with repeated motions **(1)**.

Getting the pressure and the shape of your hand just right to make this work takes lots of practice. A good way to improve your skills without damaging loads of pitchers and mugs in the process is simply to practise pulling handles from lumps of clay not attached to anything. Most people get the hang of it after doing between 100 and 200 handles, a number that with effort can be accomplished in a couple of days **(2)**. Some people choose always to pull a handle from a lump and then attach it to the pot after first making sure it will fit. When using this method, allowing the handle to stiffen up a bit by first hanging it off a table for an hour or two can make it easier to manipulate and attach **(3)**.

Once a handle has been attached to a piece, it is best to slow down the drying process somewhat to reduce the chance of the handle drying too fast and falling off. The clay of both handle and pot needs to be of a similar moisture content for the best results when attaching handles. Loosely covering the work with plastic once you have attached your handle and leaving it to dry slowly normally does the trick.

Pulling a handle off the side of a mug.

Pulling handles gets easier with practice.

Hanging your pulled handles off the edge of a table gives you a chance to review your progress.

Special shapes on the wheel: lids and spouts

Lids can be made in a variety of ways, some of which are easier than others. The simplest lid is made by opening your centred clay about halfway between the middle and the outer edge, instead of opening in the centre as you would normally do to make a bowl or a pot **(1)**. Then, the clay left in the centre can be shaped into a knob, and the clay at the edge can be formed into the lip of the lid, or just smoothed out **(2)**.

In order for this simple lid to fit the top of a thrown piece, some sort of special rim must be fashioned onto the base in order to hold the lid in place. This can be accomplished with practice once your thrown pieces are well centred and have even rims **(3)**. You must also measure carefully to get the lid to fit the pot. Use callipers or a ruler.

Dan Rhode, *Lidded Vessel*, 2003, 20 x 18cm (8 x 7 in.). Fired to cone 6 in oxidation.

Making a simple drop-in lid

Opening up a centred piece of clay off-centre to make a lid.

Shaping a simple lid.

Shaping the rim on a pot to hold a lid.

Making a lid with a flange, adding knobs and making spouts

More complicated lids can be made that require more steps. Making a lid with a flange requires starting it off upside-down. First, throw a small bowl with a bit of clay facing outwards and a bit standing up on the rim. This can be achieved by doing what is sometimes called 'splitting the lip' (**1A and 1B**). After allowing this to stiffen up (possibly overnight), turn over the small thick bowl and trim it into a dome. Then attach a knob to the top by scoring and slipping a small bit of clay onto the top (see p.60), giving this a few minutes to set up, and then shaping it back on the wheel (**2A and 2B**).

Hollow, tubular spouts are made usually for adding to a teapot, which many potters find to be a fun and challenging form to make. Unfortunately, fewer and fewer people are using teapots these days, so the market for them is not what it once was. To make the spout, open a small amount of clay part way down (**3**). Pull up a small cylinder that slopes inwards as much as your hands will allow. Then collar the cylinder inwards to make the spout (**4A, 4B and 4C**).

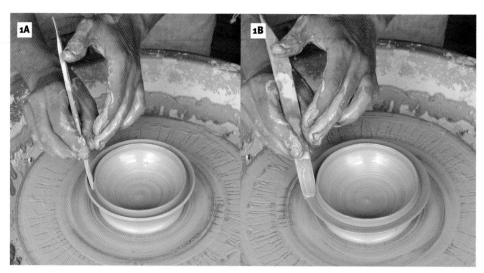

Using a wood tool to split the lip of a lid.   The bottom of the lid after shaping.

Adding a knob to the top of a leatherhard lid, by scoring and slipping.   Throwing the knob onto the lid once attached.

Opening clay to make a spout.

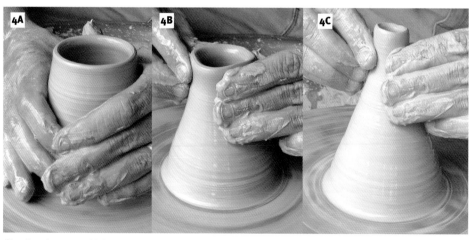

Shaping the spout. Using your hands and then your fingers as the spout gets narrower, gradually squeeze the clay in, working from bottom to top.

right The finished teapot after attaching the spout and handle.

Assembling a teapot

Take a look at the images to see the steps required to assemble a teapot. The body must first be trimmed and allowed to get stiff, then the lid made to fit, then the handle and the spout attached. There is an infinite variety of ways of making these pieces go together. See what you can come up with **(1, 2 and 3)**.

right Jennifer Siegel, *Teapot,* 20 x 15cm (8 x 6in.). Wheelthrown, glazed and fired in a gas and salt kiln in reduction. *Photo by Seth Tice-Lewis.*

Attaching the spout to the trimmed teapot.

Attaching the handle to the teapot.

Disabilities and throwing

Wheelchair-accessible wheels are available and do a good job at allowing a person with no use of their legs to make pots. They do cost a bit more, but the wheel itself is suspended on a lifting mechanism, which allows for a wheelchair to be moved in underneath and the wheel set at the correct height. Centring and throwing can be accomplished if need be with only one hand, either right or left. With the wheel turning anti-clockwise, the left hand can do all the centring by itself, as long as the left elbow is well braced. This can be done by holding the elbow against your torso, or by using one of the adjustable armrests built into most accessible wheels. Similarly, the right hand can do the centring with the wheel turning clockwise. It is imperative to use a wheel that can revolve in either direction in these circumstances, and many wheels have this capability. Even without hands, the clay can be manipulated on the wheel using forearms or elbows, even chins and cheeks, not to mention feet. There is no 'right' or 'wrong' way to make things with clay. A useful book for simple project ideas is *Clay For People With Special Needs* (see p. 158).

HANDBUILDING

Handbuilding can be a very complicated process or a very simple one. Manipulating clay with your hands is a simple, straightforward process, one that requires no technology or tools and can therefore be very rewarding. At other times very specific and refined results are required that take advantage of exacting processes. It is good to challenge yourself and try a variety of ways of working with clay in order to discover the way that you are most drawn to. Often, however, we are at the mercy of limited time and energy, so one or two specific ways of working will necessarily be our methods of 'choice'.

Whatever you choose to make, there are a few guidelines to follow that will help you achieve your goals:

1. Be aware of thickness! Most kiln-firing schedules will cause pieces to crack if they are more than 2.5cm (1in.) thick. Schedules can be adapted to allow for extra-thick pieces, but the energy spent firing kilns very slowly is often unnecessary and unwarranted.

2. Use the right clay body. Small handbuilt pieces can be made from just about any clay, but bigger pieces should be made from clay bodies with more grog or sand in them, up to about 30% by dry weight. This will help reduce cracking both during drying and firing.

3. Remember the size limitations of your kiln! If you want to make a big sculpture, consider cutting it up after construction into pieces that can fit in the kiln and then be reassembled after firing and attached with epoxy glue.

4. Consider shrinking and cracking. Clay tends to shrink 10–20% during drying and firing. The stress lines in a piece tend to be towards its centre, which is often where it is thickest and biggest. Delicate extensions away from the centre might be best made from another material, such as wood or metal, which can be added after firing. Most successful large pieces made from clay lack long appendages or are symmetrically aligned around their centre (like a pot). It is certainly true that successful pieces are made that are thin, delicate, and shaped in a way that would normally result in cracking. These pieces either take advantage of superior materials (like paperclay, see p.22) or very careful construction and long-term drying. Discuss your goals with other artists or suppliers and find out what methods and materials might work best for your more complicated work.

5. Much time and energy can be saved by working up drawings of your ideas before beginning with clay. Planning your ideas in a sketchbook before commencing or even taking a class or two in 2D and 3D design can be very helpful in generating ideas for your clay work.

6. Do not enclose a hollow space in your piece! There must be an opening into every cavity or the air inside will expand and probably cause your piece to explode during firing.

Handbuilding: Working with slabs (slab-building)

There are several basic methods for constructing things with clay. Slab-building makes use of flattened pieces of clay that are then cut up and reassembled. This method has the advantage of using pieces of clay of a uniform thickness, which helps in drying and firing. Slab-building also has the advantage of working with pieces of clay that have been allowed to partially dry and stiffen prior to assembly, making it easier to create bigger and taller pieces. Slab-built pieces can be made to look very angular and geometric, resulting in some finished pieces looking very much unlike clay.

To make a slab, most people use either a slab roller (see p.38) or a rolling pin (1). When using a rolling pin be sure to pick up the slab every few rolls so as to stop it sticking to the table top. Roll out your slabs on a table or board covered with canvas or cloth. A useful item is an old oil-cloth tablecloth which can be used cloth side up. The thickness of the slab will determine the strength of the clay and the heaviness of the finished piece. After rolling out, while the clay is still soft, it is easy to add a texture or design to the surface (2).

Most people constructing forms from rolled slabs first allow them to dry until they are 'leatherhard', a stage where the clay can still be easily carved but is not floppy. Assembling slabs into a form then requires the shapes to be cut much like a fabric artist might cut cloth, though in this case the cutting will be done with a fettling knife or a needle tool (3). The slabs can then be assembled into any shape you wish. The slabs then behave a little like cardboard. To assemble and join your slabs together, the edges must first be scored with a fork, needle tool or serrated rib, and then slip (sloppy, wet clay) is applied with a brush to act as a

Rolling an even slab with a rolling pin takes practice.

Adding some texture to a slab using a home-made tool.

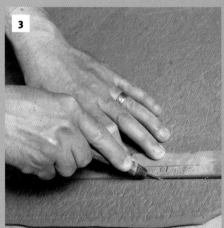

Use a straight edge and a needle tool or clay knife to cut shapes from a leatherhard slab.

Cathy Kiffney at work in her studio, which doubles as a display area for her work. *Photo by the artist.*

In preparation for attaching slabs together, first score along the edges.

Handbuilding: Working with slabs continued

Then apply slip to the scored edges.

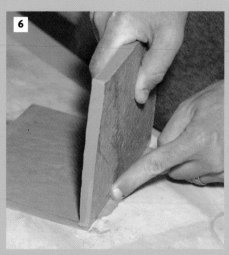

Push the slabs together firmly to force any trapped air out.

Adding a coil to the inside of a slab seam makes it much stronger.

glue to keep the slabs together. This is known as scoring and slipping (4, 5 and 6). For larger forms, adding a coil of clay along the inside edge can help increase strength and decrease the likelihood of cracking (7). After all the slabs are joined together, the finished piece is allowed to dry out slowly under plastic for several days. This helps to balance the moisture content and avoid cracks (8).

above Linda Caswell, *Porcelain Agateware Bowl*, 2003, dia: 20cm (8in.). To make this agateware, the colours are in the clay itself, not a surface decoration. The colourants are added to separate pieces of porcelain, which are then shaped and rolled together; the resulting slab is draped over a hump mould. *Photo by the artist.*

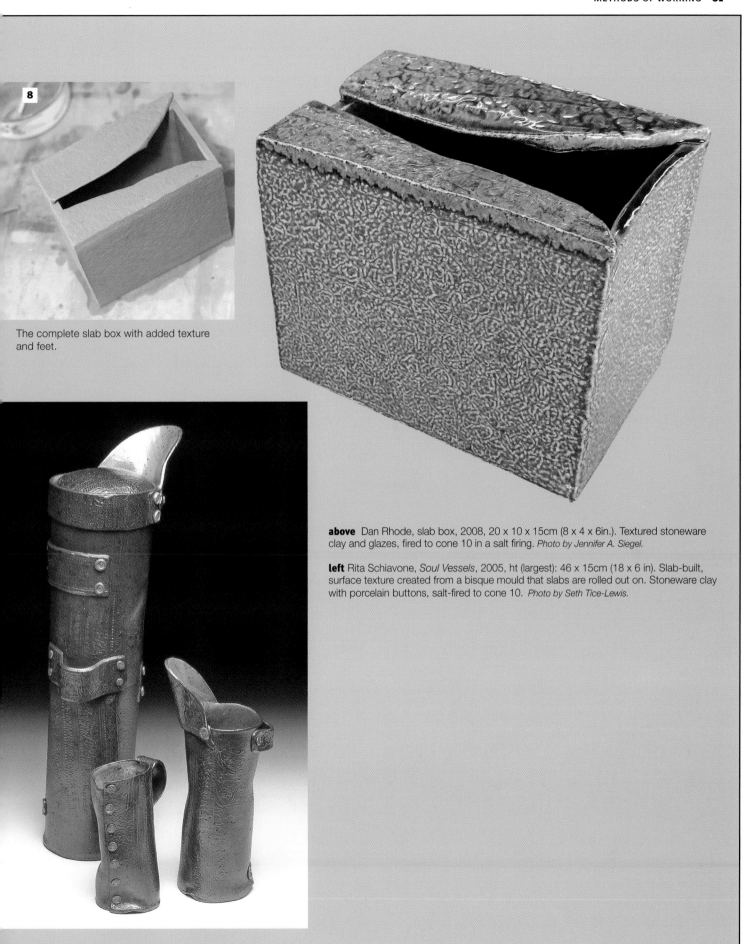

8

The complete slab box with added texture and feet.

above Dan Rhode, slab box, 2008, 20 x 10 x 15cm (8 x 4 x 6in.). Textured stoneware clay and glazes, fired to cone 10 in a salt firing. *Photo by Jennifer A. Siegel.*

left Rita Schiavone, *Soul Vessels*, 2005, ht (largest): 46 x 15cm (18 x 6 in). Slab-built, surface texture created from a bisque mould that slabs are rolled out on. Stoneware clay with porcelain buttons, salt-fired to cone 10. *Photo by Seth Tice-Lewis.*

Handbuilding: Working with coils (coil-building)

Coil-building makes use of rolled-out 'ropes' or 'coils' of clay that are merged together while building pieces. These pieces can be built in stages, allowing lower portions to dry out and stiffen before subsequent layers are added. Coils can be made of any thickness, depending on the strength required in the area being constructed. Coil-built pieces tend to be flowing, curvy pieces without many angles or straight lines.

To make coils, get a lump of clay and squeeze it in your hands into a rough, thick coil **(1)**.

Next, roll the clay back and forth on a flat surface. The clay will usually acquire a flattened side during rolling, and the best way to correct this is to stop periodically and simply pat it round again. Your ability to roll long, even coils will improve with practice **(2)**.

Preparing a piece of clay for rolling into a coil.

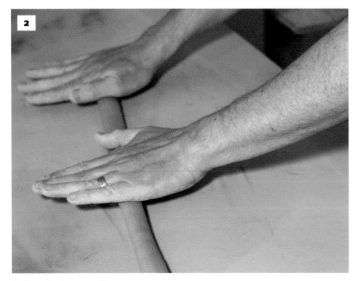

Rolling clay into a coil.

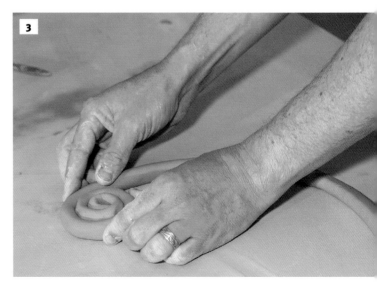

Beginning a coil pot.

As scoring and slipping long coils together can be tedious, most people working with coils simply smooth them together as they go, thus obviating the need to score and slip **(3, 4 and 5)**. If you are not scoring and slipping your coils, you need to make sure your clay is flexible and plastic enough to do this. If tiny cracks appear in your coils when you bend them, then they may not be damp and soft enough to use without slip.

As the coil-built pot stiffens after building, it can be shaped and smoothed with ribs and other tools into the finished form **(6)**.

right Coil pot after glazing and firing.
Photo by Jennifer A. Siegel.

The pot grows after adding a few more coils.

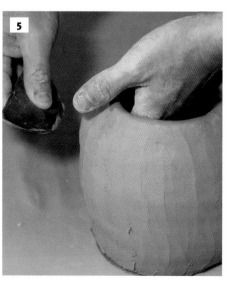

Smoothing the coils with a rib.

Coil pot after shaping.

THROWING AND ALTERING

Many artists use the wheel to create initial forms that they then spend a lot of time changing. Handbuilt pieces of clay are added, parts are cut off, and textures and stamps can be used to create objects that are no longer even remotely round! This combination of processes is hugely popular and the results are all around us. Next time you are at a ceramics show, see if you can identify the various techniques that were required to make the pieces you see. Be sure to ask questions of the artists, as they are typically more than happy to assist you in developing your own methods.

CLAY RECYCLING

Do not throw away your scraps! Reuse your clay as much as possible as this will not only save resources and time, it will also be an illustrative process for learning about what clay can do and how it behaves (or misbehaves). Clay from purchased bags of clay is not ruined after it becomes hard and dry or wet and squishy. All you need to do is spend some time getting it back to the right consistency for use again. Here are some steps to follow (see opposite). One important point is to make sure you keep different types of clay separate as you go along, for recycling later.

right Jennifer Lawler-Mecca, *Twin Vases*, 2008, 25.5 x 18 x 10cm (10 x 7 x 4in.). Thrown in parts and assembled. *Photo by Randy McNeilly.*

Beginning to mix the clay by hand; breaking up any large lumps.

How to recycle

1. Collect all your scraps, wet and dry, in a bucket. It is often easier to collect a whole bunch before recycling than to recycle little bits at a time, but circumstances often dictate the regularity with which recycling needs to occur.

2. Make sure the scrap collection bucket is topped up with water to turn your clay into as soupy and gloopy a mess as you can make. Your bucket can sit as long as you need it to. There is no time limit for storing used clay. However, you must let any completely dry clay become wet again before proceeding; this usually happens in a matter of hours.

3. When ready to recycle, first remove as much standing water from the top of the bucket as you can, using a scoop or a sponge. Then roll up your sleeves and dive in! Use your hands like mixers, squeezing and mixing all the clay together as best you can. The main thing you want to do is break up any large clumps of firm wet clay. Just squeezing it through your fingers a few times is enough; it does not have to become consistently creamy and smooth.

4. Now is when it is best to have a wedging board made from plaster on hand, onto which you will spread the clay. Spread it thick, about 5–10cm (2–4in.). If your plaster is allowed to completely dry between batches, it will help pull water out of the clay quickly. Putting the clay in front of a fan or in the sun will also speed up the process. Equally, you can spread the clay out on cement or a rock. Spreading the clay out on a board or a cloth will work as well, though you may also end up with a serious rot/mould problem that will render the board or cloth useless after several goes.

5. Check to see if the clay is ready. Depending on your situation this may take hours, days or even weeks.

Very large amounts of clay spread out on a non-porous surface can take a long time to become dry enough to use again. Sometimes the edges are ready first. Keep testing it and comparing your recycled clay to the clay that you like to use for your projects. In this regard there are two tests that can help take the guesswork out of this process.

The first is the splat test. Take a ball of your recycled clay and a ball of the same size of your known good clay and hold each one as high as you can over a hard floor. Drop each and compare how big they have become, how much they have splatted against the floor. If they look the same, then they are probably of a similar moisture content and your recycled clay is ready.

The second test uses a penetrometer, which you will have to construct yourself as they are not commonly sold and are easy to make. Take a thin metal bar or pipe about a foot long and mark graduations on the side starting from one end. Then, holding this bar up as high as you can, first drop it end first into your recycled clay and then into your known good clay. Compare how far it penetrated the clay. If the penetrations are nearly the same, then your recycled clay is ready.

6. Wedge your recycled clay for a good few minutes to make sure it is completely mixed, then get back to work! See the next section on how to wedge.

WEDGING CLAY

Different people have wildly varying ideas about how important and useful it is to wedge clay before using it. For some, it is like a religious experience. They believe that wedging brings life and energy to the clay, as well as aligning the particles and getting it 'ready' for use. Others think it is a waste of time and energy and should be avoided whenever possible. For starters, it should be said that working with clay can be hard on your body, and wedging clay is doubtless one of the activities most likely to aggravate an existing shoulder, elbow, wrist or hand condition. If you suffer from arthritis, tendonitis or carpal tunnel syndrome, then wedging should probably be avoided as much as is practical. On the other hand, if you are looking for a free upper-body workout, then wedge away!

Generally, clay that is purchased premixed in a bag is considered by many to be ready to go and requires no wedging. But recycled clay will always

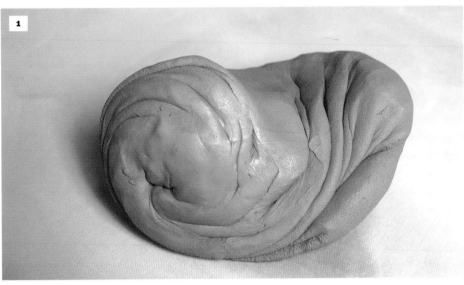

Wedging into a cone shape, using the coning or spiral method.

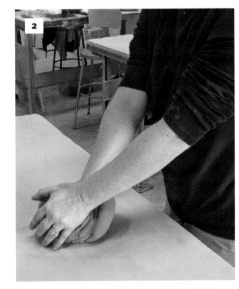

Wedging clay using the cone shape method.

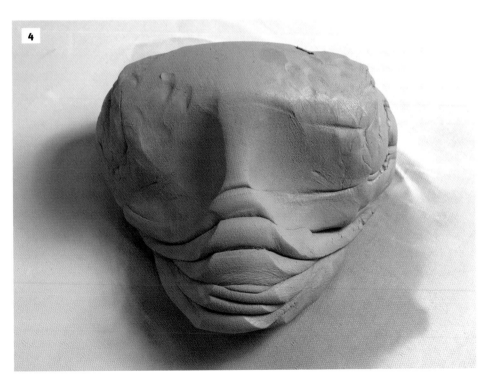

Wedging into a ram's head.

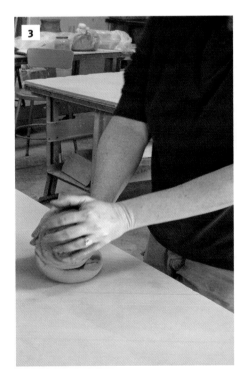

The clay is lifted and turned slightly each time.

require some wedging to get the air out and complete the mixing process. However, if you happen to own a de-airing pug mill then you will be able to have a machine do your recycled-clay wedging for you (See p. 37).

Wedging is a process whereby clay is purposefully and carefully blended back into itself in order to end up with a clay that is homogeneous (well mixed) and air-pocket (bubble) free. There are a variety of methods by which this can be accomplished, and no two people wedge in exactly the same way. The best way to learn is to watch someone else and mimic their moves. If that is not possible, then follow these moves:

Step 1. It is often easier to wedge a somewhat larger piece of clay all at once and then cut it into smaller pieces for your use. Most people find wedging 3–5lb (1.4–2.2kg) of clay at a go to be a reasonable amount.

Step 2. Your goal is to squish and stretch the clay without folding it, since folding will be likely to trap air in between the layers. The squishing mixes the clay and the stretching forces out air bubbles. This double action can be accomplished through a repeated short downward and outward pushing of the hands against the clay. The movement is along the lines of giving chest compressions to someone in cardiac arrest. Short, quick and repeated motions are best. You want the clay to remain in a lump and not spread out into a thin sheet, as thin sheets require folding to bring them back together.

Step 3. Some people prefer to turn the clay with one hand while pushing down with the other see image **2–3**). This will result in a cone-shaped piece of clay that is ready for the wheel (see image **1**).

Others tend to push down with both hands side by side for a few moves, then flip and turn the piece back up again to keep it from getting too spread out. This will result in a 'ram's head' (see image **4**). Try not to fold it when you do this.

Step 4. While wedging, many people like to cut through the clay with a static wire tool mounted on a table. You can do the same with a handheld wire tool, the idea being that when you cut through the clay you can see inside and look for non-mixed areas or bubbles. If you find bubbles or lumps, keep on wedging, and then try cutting it again. Also, cutting it is a little like cutting a deck of cards: you get a new part on top and bottom, which helps with the mixing.

Step 5. It is difficult to know for sure when you have wedged enough. There is no way to detect from the outside if there are any tiny air bubbles left inside. The best test is to use the wire cutting tool as in step 4. You will soon see any small spaces on the surface of the clay – air bubbles. After using some of your wedged clay you will find out if it still has a habit of hiding bubbles. If it does then simply increase the amount of time you spend wedging your clay before you use it. If you do find some bubbles while you are working, either throwing or handbuilding, if the bubbles are small you can pop them with a needle tool and keep working; larger air pockets might need to be filled in, or you may even need to start all over again. It is often the case that if you find one large air bubble you will find others, so it is best to stop before you spend hours making something only to have it explode or crack in the kiln due to trapped air.

While wedging, you can add a new material to your clay body if you want. This is a good time to add a colourant, another type of clay or a grog to the body. If wedging in dry ingredients, wear a dust mask. If adding a colourant that you know to be hazardous (see the list in Chapter 2, p. 26) then be sure also to wear thin rubber gloves.

SAFETY

The most common injuries in many ceramic studios are cuts on fingertips from broken glaze found on the bottom of pots where the glaze has run onto a kiln shelf. Keep a careful eye on pieces coming out of the kilns and set aside carefully those where the glaze has run down the sides and made contact with the kiln shelf. More information on kiln safety will be included in the chapter on kilns.

Dust in the studio must be maintained at low levels. Breathing airborne clay-dust particles poses a health risk over time. Silicosis and bronchitis can be triggered by prolonged inhalation of clay dust. Potentially more dangerous in the short term is breathing dust particles from hazardous glaze materials, usually those ingredients used to colour glazes. Always wear a dust mask rated at N95 when working with dry glaze ingredients.

Pay attention when using your wheel! There is always a risk of electric shock when water and electricity are close together. If your wheel is electric keep the plug up off the floor and make sure your socket outlet is RCD-protected in the UK and GFCI-protected in the US. Also remember that wheels are powerful tools. Be very careful to avoid loose clothing, jewellery, hair, or loose apron strings getting wrapped around any moving part.

Ergonomics are an important and sometimes overlooked aspect of safety in the art studio. If you spend long hours working, be sure to switch between tasks regularly; do not do the same task hour after hour. Try to get your wheel and tables at the correct height for your body. Use good body mechanics when wedging and lifting and when loading or unloading your kiln.

See the health and safety section at the end of the book for more information on safety.

4

HEATWORK AND FIRING CLAY

HEATWORK:
the relationship between temperature and time

People with an interest in ceramics and kilns will often ask clay artists about the temperature a piece of work was fired to. Usually, the person who made it can only give them a rough estimate of temperature. More accurately, however, the maker will reply not with a temperature but with a 'cone' measurement. To the beginner this can sound a bit confusing and annoying. Why can't potters just simply talk about temperature and stay away from dealing with 'cones'? Aren't they just making something simple into something more complicated?

Not at all! When firing pottery, and for that matter when baking cookies, temperature is only half (or less!) of the equation that describes how the piece was heated. For example, in the case of baking cookies, recipes will normally specify what temperature the cookies should be baked at as well as how long they should be baked. The recipe

usually indicates that the oven should be preheated before the raw dough is put in. The preheating part of the recipe does not benefit the cookies so much as it ensures that the recipe will work; not all ovens heat up at the same speed, so recipes cannot accurately indicate how long to bake the cookies when starting with a cold oven.

Theoretically, clay artists could also start with preheated kilns. Then they could follow a recipe for firing their kiln that involved putting the pieces in for a certain length of time, and then pulling them out, just as one does with cookies. The problem is that the process would become life-threatening as the heat given off by an open kiln at 1100°C (2012°F) is considerably more intense than that given off by an oven at 160°C (320°F) not to mention that the pieces would probably crack from the thermal shock. So, to avoid a massively painful and ultimately disappointing experience, all ceramic artists (with the possible exception of raku artists) load their kilns when they are cold, heat them up, then cool them back down before unloading.

Therefore, 'recipes' for 'cooking' pots are necessarily more complicated than oven recipes, as they have to take into account the warming up of the kiln as it approaches its peak temperature, and the cooling down that follows.

The firing of the pieces – meaning the physical and chemical changes that occur to each piece in the kiln – begins to happen at relatively low temperatures. The work done by the heat of the kiln begins with the drying-out of the pieces, followed by the burning-off of any organic material. After this point, more complex changes occur to the clay (and glazes) of the piece, which can result in a vitrified pot with a glassy glaze surface.

Heatwork, then, can be defined as the sum total of all the effects that heat has had on the pieces in the kiln over the duration of the firing. This 'total amount of work' idea is more succinctly summed up in the term 'cone'. The term is therefore an indication of how much heat has been delivered to an object over time.

The word 'cone' comes from the use of small cone-shaped pieces of clay that

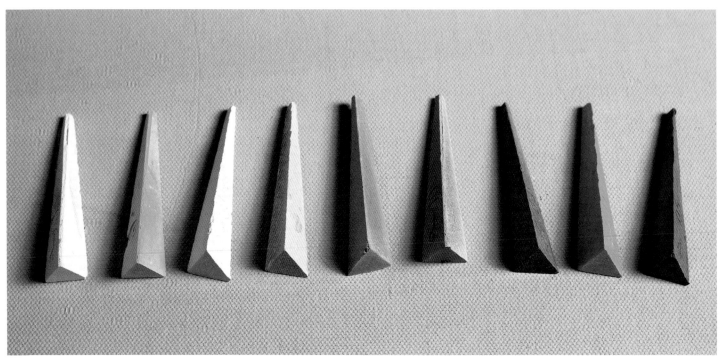

Pyrometric cones are colour-coded to help distinguish between them during handling.

The cone packs in this kiln after firing can be seen in the bottom middle of the image. In the cone pack nearest the bottom of the image, the cones have completely melted and turned to glass. *Photo by Jennifer A. Siegel.*

A kiln sitter.

are used to demonstrate the amount of heatwork achieved in a firing. There are many different cone values. Most potters and clay artists use cones with values from 022 to 12. Cone values with a zero at the front of the number count backwards and indicate lower cone values than ones without (cone 012 is a lower cone than cone 12).Cone 022 indicates temperatures in the range of about 1000–1200°F (550–650°C), whereas cone 12 is associated with temperatures in the range of about 2300–2500°F (1250–1400°C). Industries working with very high temperatures identify cone values up to about 40. See the table on p.154 for a list of cone values.

WHAT IS A 'CONE'?

Pyrometric cones are small, cone-shaped pieces of clay. They are manufactured using precise ingredients to ensure that they will soften and melt at the cone value stamped on them. They are considered the most accurate way of measuring heat work done in a kiln; they are more accurate than a pyrometer.

Some kilns use cones in a mechanism called a 'kiln sitter', which actually shuts the kiln off when the desired cone softens. Otherwise, many potters put 'cone packs' in their kilns and keep an eye on them (using great caution!) through a spy hole, which allows them to monitor the stages of the firing and assess its completeness.

phenomenon is described in the table on p.154 at the end of the book, where each cone value is given three peak-temperature values depending on the rate of heating.

Clearly, the concepts of 'cone' and 'heatwork' have their limits. A piece of pottery sitting at room temperature forever will still never reach cone 6. Likewise, a kiln at 1,000,000 degrees will never successfully fire a pot in a few seconds. The peak temperature suitable for firing clay to a specific cone will normally be within a range of a few hundred degrees, depending on the schedule. Choosing the best one for you will depend on a variety of factors having to do with the pieces you are making and the limitations of your kiln. More information about firing schedules will be covered in Chapter 10.

left Noah Riedel, *3CUPS Beer Stein*, 2008, 15 x 13 x 10cm (6 x 5¼ x 4 in.). Single-fired to cone 7. *Photo by Seth Tice-Lewis.*

below A graph depicting different firing schedules which all achieve the same cone value in different ways.

The most important concept to understand about cones is that there are many different firing schedules that can be followed to achieve the very same cone value. The graph (right) illustrates this point. Each line on the graph depicts a theoretical different firing schedule that results in the same cone value! As you can see, the peak temperature achieved relates to the speed at which the temperature rose during the firing. Faster temperature increases (less time) require higher peak temperatures (more heat) to achieve the same results. This same

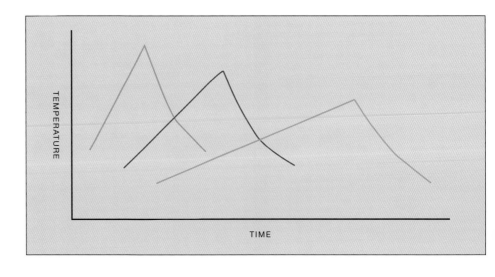

TEMPERATURE

TIME

WHAT HAPPENS TO CLAY WHEN IT IS FIRED?

Clay and glazes go through a number of changes during a typical firing. Not all firings are the same: some firings take unfired clay nearly to its melting point (and hopefully not further than this!), while others might just be intended to fuse an enamel or lustre onto the surface of a glaze. Bisque and raku firings tend to be to lower cones than earthenware and stoneware firings. The following description will be for a theoretical firing where the clay has not been fired before. See Chapter 10 for more detailed information on how to fire kilns.

Stage 1. At the lowest firing temperatures, the process of drying the clay continues. Atmospheric moisture is driven off up to the boiling temperature of water, 100°C (212°F). It is important not to heat up the kiln too quickly past this temperature, as clay explosions can occur! As the water turns to steam it expands dramatically, so only perfectly dry pieces will survive the firing past this point. Kilns are often set at a low setting, spy holes are left open and lids are left ajar for several hours to allow this moisture to come out of the kiln and not to condense on the inside of the kiln's shell or, worse still, electronic equipment.

A kiln lid propped open to allow steam to escape.

Stage 2. Between 260°C (500°F) and 480°C (900°F) the chemically bound water is driven out of clay. This is the water that actually forms the molecules of kaolin that gives wet clay the characteristics useful to artists (see Chapter 2, p.24). Once this water is driven off as steam, the clay objects have turned into ceramic objects and will no longer disintegrate in water.

Stage 3. Starting at about 420°C (800°F) any organic material in the clay begins to burn. This continues to above 820°C (1500°F). Depending on the kind and amount of material present, it is possible to see smoke being emitted from the kiln. If firing proceeds too quickly through this stage, bloating can occur as expanding gases (mostly carbon dioxide) attempt to exit the clay too quickly.

Stage 4. At 573°C (1063°F) the clay goes through a physical change to its molecular structure, commonly called a quartz inversion. The silica molecules change shape, actually getting about 2% bigger during heating and 2% smaller upon cooling (if they have not melted into glass). If this temperature is passed too quickly, cracks can develop, especially in weak areas of the pieces such as rims.

Stage 5. Not much more happens to the clay until it reaches about 1000°C (1800°F). At this point, vitrification begins as the most readily fusible oxides of the clay body begin to melt. This process continues as time or temperature increases, and will cease either when the kiln cools sufficiently or the piece completely liquefies, which for most clays is well above 1200°C (2200°F).

Clay artists are usually interested in getting their pieces to vitrify to some extent in order to make the pieces hard, durable and impermeable to water and oil. Ceramic artists making pieces for non-functional purposes may have little interest in the extent to which their pieces vitrify and may be happy with a clay that is nearly entirely unvitrified. Unvitrified fired clays are often described as porous or 'open'.

Most kiln operators set their kilns or monitor their firings such that only a partial melting within their pieces occurs, leaving them with hardened, durable pots. The people responsible for paying for the kilns hope that only the glazes will be allowed to melt completely, and not the pots!

Upon cooling, the melted oxides harden to form glass within the pieces. Slow cooling will allow crystals to develop, which can influence both the appearance of the glazes on the surface and the strength of the fired clay body. Fast cooling can be done as well, to limit the growth of crystals, often with no ill effects.

SAFETY: FUMES AND VENTILATION

During a firing, many different types of fumes are emitted. Be sure to read up on the details of kiln safety found in Chapter 10 (p.124) and in the health and safety section at the end of the book (pp.155–6).

A warning sign above some electric kilns.

5

GLAZES:
Components,
Chemistry
and Fired
Characteristics

RAW MATERIALS USED IN GLAZES

An awful lot can be said about the various materials commonly used in ceramic glazes. Most materials that are available to ceramic artists can be purchased from a supplier in the form of a powder. Many of the powders are white and appear to be identical. The important differences between them come at their atomic level.

Don't worry! To be a ceramic artist you do not need a background in chemistry! However, coming to grips with some basic chemistry as it relates to your artistic medium will help you understand what is happening during the drying and firing of your pieces. It will also help you make better things, so it is worth understanding.

Many materials used in glazes are the same as those used to make clay bodies (see p. 27). In fact, the difference between a clay body and a glaze is often just the proportion of materials used, and the amount of water added to the mix. The table above lists two recipes: the recipe on the left will make a cone 10 glaze, the recipe on the right will make a cone 10 clay body.

Another way of looking at the similarity between clay bodies and glazes is to think about what happens at different firing temperatures. A given clay body that fires well at earthenware temperatures might melt into a puddle at stoneware temperatures (see p.p.32–3). Therefore, this low-fire clay body might work well as a high-fire glaze simply by blending it up with some water and applying it to the surface of a stoneware pot. Many iron-rich reddish or brown clays found in the wild behave this way.

	Recipe 1	Recipe 2
Wollastonite	23	5
Talc	14	5
Kaolin	10	35
Ball clay	5	10
Stoneware clay	30	40
Silica	18	5
Total	100	100

A glaze made from recipe 1 and a test tile made from recipe 2. *Photo by Jennifer A. Siegel.*

Try This!

A glaze made from clay

Take a ball of a red-earthenware clay body, allow it to dry completely, and drop it into the bottom of a small test bowl made from a stoneware clay. Fire to stoneware temperatures and see if the earthenware ball 'glazed' the bottom of the bowl. If not, try mixing in a small amount of a feldspar with the wet earthenware before it dries, and then do the same test again.

The main idea to understand at this point is that clays and glazes are essentially the same thing! A clay body can be changed into a glaze by (1) firing to a higher cone, (2) re-proportioning the materials already in the clay body, or (3) adding a few additional ingredients.

Raw materials used in glazes fall into the following categories:

Clays
Feldspars
Frits
Flux-oxide sourcing materials
Colourants

Depending on where you live, your local supplier will be able to supply you with mined or quarried materials specific to your country or area, as well as some materials not available locally that will be shipped in from around the world.

The **clays** used to make glazes and clay bodies fall into two groups: primary (kaolins) and secondary (ball clays), (see also p.18). Kaolins tend to be characterised by their purity – they tend to be whiter (less iron) but coarser. Ball clays tend to be grey or red in colour due to the iron present in them, and they tend to be finer and stickier (easier to roll up into a 'ball'!) Clays all have different characteristics due to a wide array of 'contaminating' ingredients found in them, only one of which is the aforementioned iron. However, the main two oxides that clays contain (as discussed in Chapter 2) are silica and alumina. More information about oxides is provided in the following section.

Like clay, **feldspars** are all made up primarily of two oxides, silica and alumina, but unlike clays they also contain a significant amount of a third oxide: a flux! A flux is a compound that lowers the melting point of silica during a firing. The flux oxides in feldspars vary but they are normally either sodium, potassium or lithium.

Frits can be thought of as manmade feldspars. They are designed to contain certain proportions of silica, alumina and a wider variety of flux oxides than is found in naturally occurring feldspars. Sold under a variety of trade names, there are lots to choose from (see table 5 – in the section on technical information on p.153 – for chemical analyses of various frits and feldspars).

Flux-oxide sourcing materials include (see Table 4 in the section on technical

information at the end of the book on p. 152 for more detailed information):

Barium carbonate
Bone ash
Dolomite
Gerstley borate
Lithium carbonate
Magnesium carbonate
Soda ash
Strontium carbonate
Talc
Volcanic ash
Whiting
Wood ash
Zinc oxide

While some of these are also a source of alumina and silica – and are therefore similar to feldspars – they are primarily used in a glaze for the flux oxides they contain.

There are many different **colourants** that can be used in ceramic glazes, in combination or alone, and among them

are materials that variegate a glaze and others that make a glaze opaque (see the notes to table 3 in the section on technical information at the end of the book). Some of these materials are naturally occurring substances: cobalt carbonate, cobalt oxide, copper carbonate, red iron oxide, tin oxide, crocus martis, chrome oxide, iron chromate, manganese dioxide, nickel oxide, rutile, zirconium oxide and yellow ochre.

There is also a huge variety of manmade colourants to choose from, made up of combinations of these raw materials. These are often referred to as glaze stains or mason stains and are identified by number. Getting familiar with which ones develop colours of interest in your work can take time. Include a variety of colourants in your repertoire as an artist, but keep in mind the health hazards of coming into contact with these substances, and the food hazards that might result if the base glaze you

Some naturally occurring colourants: chrome oxide, nickel oxide, yellow ochre, black copper oxide and red iron oxide. *Photo by Jennifer A. Siegel.*

Mason stains. *Photo by Jennifer A. Siegel.*

add them to is not leach-proof. Getting the colour you want in a glaze will be discussed further in the 'Colour response' section later in this chapter.

(See Table 4 in the section on technical information at the end of the book for a more detailed list of materials used in glazes and some of their characteristics.)

OXIDES

Fired clays and glazes are both chemical mixtures of (mostly) oxides, which are a particular kind of molecule (group of atoms) containing one or more oxygen atoms (chemical symbol 'O').

Here is a list of some of the more common oxides (and their chemical symbols) commonly used in ceramics to create glazes:

Aluminium oxide (alumina)	Al_2O_3
Barium oxide	BaO
Boric oxide	B_2O_3
Calcium oxide	CaO
Lead oxide	PbO
Lithium oxide	Li_2O
Magnesium oxide	MgO
Potassium oxide	K_2O
Silicon Dioxide (silica)	SiO_2
Sodium oxide	Na_2O
Strontium oxide	SrO
Zinc oxide	ZnO

In the list above, the chemical symbols are given for the atoms in the molecule. The numbers following the symbols – as in Al for aluminium at the top of the list which is followed by a $_2$ – simply indicate the number of that kind of atom in the molecule. This specificity is of little importance to ceramic artists, but is included here for accuracy. At high temperatures silica melts and combines with other oxides, and upon cooling the mixture of oxides hardens and forms glaze. A finished, cooled glaze is a recombination of the atoms found in the raw materials from which it was made.

It is interesting to note how similar glass (as in window or bottle glass) and ceramic glazes really are. The only real difference between glass and glaze is in how the material behaves when melted: glass needs to be quite runny in order to be poured into a form or spread out into a sheet; glazes need to be more viscous when melted, which allows them to stay on the pottery surface and not flow off.

The roles played by oxides

As we have seen, a variety of oxides can be found in any given glaze. Some glazes contain many, others few. However, nearly all ceramic glazes will contain three categories of oxides:

glass formers
stabilisers
fluxes

Silica (a shortened term for silicon dioxide or SiO_2) is the basic building block of glass, glazes and clay. It is the only oxide in the **glass former** category, and can be found in just about every ceramic glaze ever made.

Lucky for us, our second category is just as simple as the first. **Alumina** (a shortened term for aluminium oxide, or Al_2O_3) is classified as a **stabiliser** and is again the only oxide found in its category. When a glaze is melting at high temp-erature, the alumina helps to keep it viscous, ensuring that it does not run right off the pot like water. Therefore, alumina is found to some extent in nearly all ceramic glazes. Moreover, because alumina stiffens the melt of oxides and reduces their ability to organise into crystals, alumina in the right proportion helps to ensure an amorphous blend of oxides that give a glaze a translucent and uniform appearance. Ceramic glazes low or lacking in alumina often develop crystals. Indeed, by manipulating the amount of alumina, glazes can be created that will grow micro and macro crystals, creating fantastic effects (see p.24).

The third and last category of oxides, the **fluxes**, is quite a bit more complex than the first two. All of these oxides have the property of fluxing silica, helping it to melt at a lower temperature. It is also interesting that the presence of silica in return helps to melt many of these fluxing oxides at lower temperatures than they would melt at by themselves. When this symbiotic fluxing relationship is maximised – meaning, when the two materials are in the right proportion to each other to maximise melting – it is called the eutectic point for that mixture.

Here is a list categorising the three types of oxides used in making glazes:

Glass formers
Silica SiO_2

Stabilisers
Alumina Al_2O_3

Fluxes
Barium oxide	BaO
Boric oxide	B_2O_3
Calcium oxide	CaO
Lead oxide	PbO
Lithium oxide	Li_2O
Magnesium oxide	MgO
Potassium oxide (potash)	K_2O
Sodium oxide (soda)	Na_2O
Strontium oxide	SrO
Zinc oxide	ZnO

All ceramic glazes have at least two of these oxides (silica and a flux) and nearly all of them have three or more, including alumina and at least one other flux. Many base glazes (meaning, glazes without colourants) contain seven, eight, nine or more oxides, giving them a complex chemistry resulting in a specific set of characteristics. The next section covers some of the characteristics that we as clay artists are interested in achieving, and indicates which of these oxides might help deliver these qualities.

GLAZE HARDNESS AND DURABILITY

The ability of a glaze to withstand mechanical degradation is important mostly to potters making functional ware, but also occasionally to sculptural artists whose work will be touched, moved, or constantly subjected to flowing water. Glazes containing high proportions of calcium oxide and magnesium oxide tend to hold up the best. Glazes with high proportions of potassium, sodium, lead and boric oxides tend to have softer and more easily damaged surfaces.

COLOUR RESPONSE

Most ceramic artists find it a fairly easy task to end up with dull, muted, muddy colours on their pieces, while ending up with bright, crisp colours can be difficult. Many times the colour palette available to the artist is predetermined by the oxides lurking, silent and unseen, in the base glaze they use. The wrong oxides in a glaze will render some of the strongest colourants dull and muted, while other oxides in combination with the same colourants will give a bright and bold response. Generally speaking, the glaze oxides that tend toward bright colours are potassium, sodium, lithium, boric, barium and lead oxides.

Oxides of magnesium, calcium, strontium and zinc tend to give a duller colour response.

The presence of alumina generally dulls colours, but being a necessary oxide in most glazes its presence cannot be avoided, only limited through careful formulation (see table 3 in the section on technical information at the end of the book, p.151).

The flux oxides in a glaze can change the appearance of some colourants dramatically. Copper in a glaze normally tints the glaze green, but with the presence of lithium and barium can result in a blue glaze.

Copper carbonate is duller on the left tile than the right in part due to the oxides present: the left is high in calcium whereas the right is high in sodium and potassium. *Photo by Jennifer A. Siegel.*

top Copper can change colour dramatically as a result of the flux oxides in the glaze. On the left, the copper is in a glaze high in lithium oxide; in the middle, a glaze high in calcium oxide; and on the right, a glaze high in barium oxide. *Photo by Jennifer A. Siegel.*

above Both of these glazes have 5% iron oxide in them. The one on the left is high in strontium oxide; the one on the right is high in sodium oxide. *Photo by Jennifer A. Siegel.*

Helpful hint

Determining which ingredients to include in a glaze can be tricky. In order to develop a successful glaze you have to be prepared to be patient and ready to do as many tests as are needed. Get in the habit of including test tiles in all of your glaze firings, just to keep yourself moving forward with your glaze ingredient education! A lot of information about colour development and variegation can be found in Table 3 *Flux Oxide Colour Response* and Table 4 *Typical Amounts of Colourants to be Added to a Glaze* found at the end of this book. If you find these tables overwhelming, you are not alone! Before starting to make your own glaze, be sure to read Chapters 6 through 9. This information will help you immensely in getting started. Then, when you have all the equipment and are ready to go, dive in! But be warned: glaze testing is so much fun you might just get addicted to it. If you plan ahead, and use tiles of specific shapes, you can use all your tests eventually to create a mosaic! Be creative with your testing and don't give up; just when you think you can't make a glaze do what you want, the next test might surprise you.

Cobalt oxide usually results in a deep blue glaze, but if the glaze has a high proportion of magnesium oxide, the glaze can end up a completely different shade of blue.

The vibrancy displayed by any of the ceramic colourants will vary both by the amount of that colourant used in a glaze as well as by which oxides are present in the base glaze. A glaze with a high proportion of strontium and 5% of iron oxide will look noticeably different than 5% of iron oxide in a glaze with a high proportion of sodium (see image p.81).

Related to colour response is variegation. A few oxides tend to mix less uniformly within a glaze, resulting in a swirled or uneven appearance to the colourants blended into it. Calcium, lithium, magnesium and boric oxides are more likely than other oxides to create this mottled, uneven effect.

GLOSSY VERSUS MATT SURFACES

There are several ways to create a matt surface in a glaze. By far the most common is to simply underfire the glaze by a cone or two. The glaze does not completely melt, so some of the oxide molecules do not combine, remaining somewhat disassociated from the glass that has formed. While this method can be effective on sculpture, you would be ill-advised to create matt glazes in this way on functional pottery, as some of the underfired glaze material will come off as the piece is used, and this could pose a health threat.

Leach-resistant, stable matt glazes can be made by allowing the completely melted glaze in the kiln to grow micro-crystals. Micro-crystals break up the smooth surface of the glaze so that the eye perceives the surface as looking dry and matt. Only up close, under a microscope, can the crystals be seen. The flux oxides that best produce micro-crystals are barium, calcium, zinc, strontium and magnesium. Again, crystals grow best in a glaze low in alumina, so reducing the alumina content will help to create microcrystalline matt glazes but will also render the glaze runnier. The firing cycle used will also affect the formation of crystals (see Chapter 10).

CRAZING AND SHIVERING: GLAZE FIT

Crazing is a term used to describe small cracks that appear in a glaze after firing. Normally, a cracked glass surface on a piece is less desirable than an unbroken surface. Many pots exhibit this fault, often with no ill effects other than to their appearance. It is caused by a difference in shrinkage between the glaze and the clay body it is covering.

Most materials that melt completely will shrink far more than a similar substance that only partially melts. This explains why crazing is one of the most common glaze faults: the fully melted glaze covering the partially melted clay body shrinks more during cooling and cracks can appear. Occasionally, crazing is desirable, as when doing post-firing reduction as in raku (see Chapter 10 for a description of raku firing). The crazing cracks will pick up the smoke from the reduction and display a beautiful network of lines on the surface. Shivering is a very uncommon glaze fault where the clay body shrinks more than the glaze. Most ceramic artists never encounter this problem.

Each oxide that is used in a base glaze has a coefficient of expansion associated with it (see table 4 in the section on technical information at the

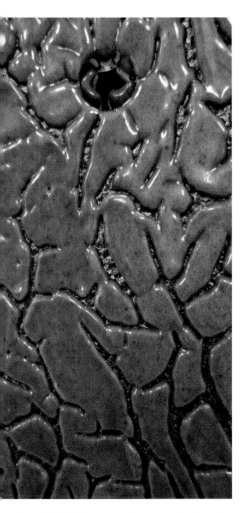

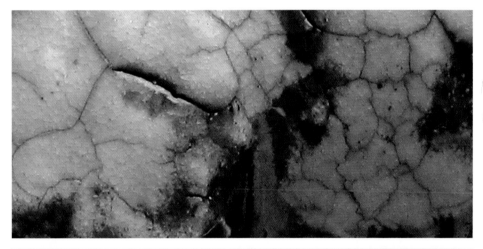

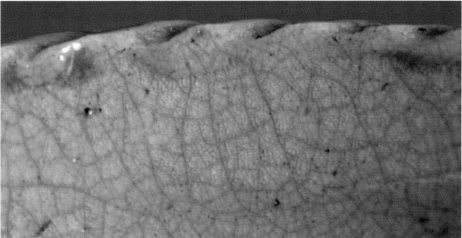

above left Detail of a crawling glaze. Crawling glazes can add an interesting surface, especially to sculptural work. This effect is usually created by applying a thick layer of glaze with an over-abundance of fine particled clay (ball clay or bentonite) in it. This clay layer usually cracks during drying, which then results in crawling during the firing. *Photo by Jennifer A. Siegel.* **top, right** Crazing can pick up the carbon during the raku process. *Photo by the author.*
bottom, right Crazing in a glaze shows up as little cracks in the surface.

end of the book). Glazes that contain oxides that expand and contract a lot tend to end up crazed. Of course, the real story here is whether or not the glaze expands and contracts more or less than the clay it is applied to. Some clay bodies expand and contract more than others, just like glazes, so getting the right glaze on the right clay body will reduce crazing to its minimum.

The flux oxides with the highest coefficients of expansion are potassium and sodium. These oxides tend to produce smooth, glossy glazes with bright colours – and crazing. At the other end of the expansion spectrum are magnesium, lithium, zinc and boric oxides. These oxides tend to produce glazes with little or no crazing. Barium, calcium and strontium oxides have coefficients of expansion in the middle of the range.

If you are having a problem with crazing, try changing your base glaze so that it contains flux oxides with lower expansion coefficients. Alternatively, you could try to vitrify (melt) your clay body a bit more. To do this, either add a bit more flux to your clay body (feldspar) or raise your firing temperature. Learning how to formulate glazes will help you make these adjustments (see Chapter 9).

below left Salinda Dahl, *Gentle,* 2005, 7.5 x 1.5cm (3 x 2½in.). Handbuilt in earthenware clay, decorated with stains, slips and glazes. *Photo by Seth Tice-Lewis.*

right Ronan Peterson, *Growth Rings Pitcher*, 30 x 20 x 15cm (12 x 8 x 6in.), wheel-thrown and altered, oxidation fired earthenware, 2008. *Photo by Tom Mills Photography.*

SAFETY: TOXICITY AND LEACHING

Safety and toxicity in ceramics is a complex area. When it comes to glazing, the most dangerous part of the process is when working with the dry materials. Inhaling dust should be avoided as much as possible. Once a glaze has been applied and fired, the resulting fired glass will fall somewhere on a scale of 'leachability', meaning some of the glazes will leach chemicals out of them more readily than others. Depending on how a glaze is used and what is in it, this can matter a whole lot or not at all. For most sculptural pieces, the leaching properties of the surface glazes are irrelevant. But on functional pottery meant to be used continuously with food, leaching of

Unstable glazes will leach colourants into food. This image shows a tile that has leached colourant after contact with lemon juice. *Photo by Jennifer A. Siegel.*

chemicals can be a big issue, though also an almost invisible one unless the potter is paying attention. Most consumers will buy ceramic ware based primarily on its visual appeal, then on its feel, and not at all on concerns over which oxides and colourants are likely to leach out into their pasta sauce!

Two aspects of toxicity need to be taken into account: first, the toxicity of the flux oxides themselves; and second, the tendency of some flux oxides to allow colourants to leach out of a glaze more easily. The flux oxides that pose a health threat themselves are those of barium, lead and lithium, and to a lesser extent boric oxide. The others, by and large, will pass through the human body with no ill effects. However, lead, potassium, sodium, barium and boric oxides do not make a durable and hard glaze, and as a result colourants in glazes with higher proportions of these oxides tend to leach more easily. It is certainly important to make sure that glazes for functional ware that rely heavily on these oxides are tested for leaching and safety. Testing can be done at home by soaking a piece of glazed pottery in lemon juice for a few days and observing whether the juice has picked up any of the glaze colour (see

image above), or else more accurately by sending your glaze off to a testing lab. For a list of testing laboratories around the world visit the Digitalfire Corporation's website at www.digitalfire.com

Another aspect relating to the safety of glazes and oxides is the cone to which the glaze is to be fired. Low-fire glazes tend to rely on a higher proportion of flux oxides than high-fire glazes. Since silica and alumina pose no health threats (once fired), the higher proportion of these to be found in high-fire glazes generally results in these glazes being safer.

The amount of a colourant added to a glaze will also have an effect on the safety of the finished ware. Of all the materials used in glazes, the colourants carry (by and large) the greatest associated health risks. John Hesselberth and Ron Roy published in 2002 a limit table in their book *Mastering Cone 6 Glazes* on how much of several common colourants should be used in a good, stable cone 6 glaze. Good, stable cone 10 glazes should be able to prevent somewhat greater percentages of these colourants from leaching, while good, stable lower-temperature glazes will be likely to leach colourants unless their percentages are

reduced (see Table 2 in the section on technical information , p.150).

Generally, to make stable, durable glazes follow these six recommendations as closely as possible (Numbers 1–3 are from *Mastering Cone 6 Glazes*. This book is mandatory reading for anyone who wants a better understanding of glaze making and formulating):

1 Keep your glaze chemistry within the unity formula limits recommended in *Mastering Cone 6 Glazes* (see Table 1, p.150).

2 Use predominantly alkaline earth fluxes – calcium oxide (CaO), magnesium oxide (MgO), strontium oxide (SrO) – or zinc oxide (ZnO) instead of alkali fluxes – sodium oxide (Na_2O), potassium oxide (K_2O), lithium oxide (Li_2O) – in your glazes. The second group tends to reduce glaze stability while the first group either helps or does not hurt stability. Limiting alkali fluxes to 25% (0.25 in unity formulas) of the total fluxes is recommended.

3 Favour a mix of fluxes instead of a heavy dependence on just one or two in a glaze.

4 Use raw materials that already contain several oxides (feldspars and frits are good choices). Using materials already made up of oxide combinations means the amount of new chemical combinations required in your firing is reduced.

5 Finer mesh sizes of any given glaze material will cause a more complete melt at a given cone value. For potentially hazardous materials purchase as fine a mesh size as possible.

6 Use the correct flux oxides in combination with your chosen colourant to get the desired colour response; this will allow you to use the least amount of potentially hazardous raw materials in your glaze.

6

MIXING GLAZES AND IMPROVING PERFORMANCE

ABOUT MIXING GLAZES

There are a variety of ways of acquiring a glaze to use on your work. The method that requires the least amount of effort on the part of the artist is simply to buy a pre-mixed glaze from a supplier. These glazes come in a variety of colours, and each is meant to be used for a specific cone value. Typically, these pre-mixed glazes are labelled as 'food-safe' or 'not food-safe' on their labels. They are also given a safety label such as 'AP Non-Toxic' or 'Health Label'. These designations pertain to the safety of the glaze once fired, not to the safety of the raw glaze. All glazes, including ones labelled 'AP Non-Toxic', should be treated as potentially toxic in their unfired state. Avoid direct contact with the glaze, and be careful of dried glaze becoming airborne – inhalation of glaze dust is one of the most insidious safety hazards in the ceramic studio.

Purchased pre-mixed glazes usually come in relatively small bottles, so application becomes an issue. Dunking, one of the most common application methods, is difficult unless a large amount of the glaze is purchased. As these pre-mixed glazes tend to be very expensive, most artists use them sparingly or not at all, preferring to mix their own to save money, and also because having your own selection of glazes is both satisfying and relatively easy to accomplish. Follow the steps described below to begin mixing glazes from recipes, and then read Chapter 9 on glaze formulation to learn about developing your own new recipes or how to fix existing glaze problems.

FINDING AND UNDER-STANDING A GLAZE RECIPE

Glaze recipes can be found in many places. Most existing studios have a variety of glazes that have been in use for years, and batches get mixed up over and over again. Recipes can be found online or in books, or can be gleaned from other artists. A few recipes for you to try are included in the section on recipes at the end of the book. Of course, the first question to be answered when searching for a recipe is, 'What cone am I firing to?' Your clay body and kiln's limits will dictate part of this answer, along with the goals you might have set for a piece of work.

The next question to answer is, 'Will this recipe do what I want?' If you are familiar with glaze-formulation software, enter the glaze into your computer for analysis and see which oxides and which amounts are present. The results will help you determine whether the glaze is likely to be food-safe, or durable, or full of cracks (crazed). A lot of poorly developed glazes can simply be skipped after looking at their formula. The more practice you have, the easier you'll find it to recognise what will or will not work. Read Chapter 9 on formulating glazes for more information.

Most glaze recipes are simply a list of materials followed by their relative amounts, which, when added up, results in a total of 100. This standard format makes changing the recipe size fairly easy. For instance, to make a 10,000 gram batch, simply multiply all the values by 100.

Next, when you have found a recipe that appears to be the right one for your purposes, determine how much of the glaze you want to mix up. If you plan to brush on a small amount, then 100–500g (3½–17½oz) of dry materials may be enough. To dip a whole platter in, you may need a big bucket and 20,000g (44lb) of powdered glaze plus water! Mostly, people use buckets for their glazes, and a 7500g (16.5lb) batch of

A large bucket of glaze suitable for dipping.

100g (3½oz) of a glaze.

Lara O'Keefe, *Covered Jar Grouping*, 2009, tallest jar: 15 x 15cm (6 x 2½in.). Wood-fired and salt-glazed, carved decoration. *Photo by Jason Dowdle.*

powdered glaze will make about 15–20l (between 4 and 5 US gal.) of liquid glaze, enough to fill the average bucket.

The first time you make a new glaze, it is advisable to make up a small batch and test it before you commit yourself, financially and otherwise, to a big batch. A 100g (3½oz) batch in a small cup is usually enough to dip a test tile in for this purpose.

Once you have determined the amount of glaze you wish to make, gather up the ingredients. Most ceramic supply stores will sell you materials by whatever weight you indicate, but will give you big discounts if you buy in bulk or buy the 'whole bag' of a material. Glaze materials by and large don't ever go bad, and they can be stored indefinitely with no ill effects. If in doubt, buy more than you need and use any leftover materials in a later batch.

Now, get together the required mixing equipment. The basics include:

- weighing scales
- a 40 or 80 mesh sieve
- a few containers to hold the glaze
- rubber gloves
- a dust mask
- sticks to stir with.

Equipment used when mixing a glaze. *Photo by Jennifer A. Siegel.*

MIXING A GLAZE

First, on a clean sheet of paper write out the amounts of all the materials you will be using. Clearly writing this out from the beginning will lessen the chance of mistakes while mixing.

Step 1. Work safely. Wear your dust mask and use an exhaust fan or work outdoors. Clean up any spilled material immediately when you have finished mixing – use a mop or a hose, but never sweep dry material as this will propel it into the air.

Step 2. Put a container on your scale and re-zero (or tare) the scale – this simply means you set the scale to zero which includes the weight of your container. It allows you to weigh your materials rather than the container the materials are in.

Weighing glaze ingredients using a digital scale.

Step 3. Scoop some of the first material in your recipe into the container on the scale **(1)**. Be as accurate as you can when you are approaching the weight you have calculated. The more accurate you are, the more likely you will be able to reproduce the results if you like them! Put this weighed material into your empty glaze container. This could be a plastic cup, a mop bucket or a clean rubbish bin! The scale of the project will depend on your goals.

    Continue to weigh out materials on the recipe and add them dry into your glaze container. Check off the materials as you go to help reduce errors. Double-check each material before you place it in with the others.

All the weighed dry materials before mixing.

Step 4. When all the materials are weighed and in a container **(2)**, stir them with a stick while still dry to mix them together. Gradually add water to the dry ingredients while stirring. (Some prefer to add the dry ingredients to a pre-measured amount of water. This is fine, and can result in fewer lumps, but be very careful NOT to start with too much water.) Continue to add water and stir until the glaze gets to a thick, soup-like but stirable consistency.

Pouring the glaze through a sieve the first time.

compare weights. If the new batch weighs more, add water to it and weigh again until they are equal; water alone added to the glaze will reduce the weight of your volume as water is less dense than the glaze particles floating around in it. You can take this measurement and determine the specific gravity of the glaze as well if you choose. Simply divide your glaze weight by the weight of the same volume of plain water. Be sure to save your cup with the mark on it or your specific-gravity results for the next time you mix each glaze. Each separate glaze you make might have a slightly different consistency requirement to produce the results you are looking for.

Step 7. Glazes tend to keep getting thicker for the first several days after mixing as the finest dry particles slowly absorb water. If you mix a glaze on Monday and come back on Tuesday and find it too thick, just add more water until it's right. Usually, this gradual thickening stops after three days.

That's it! Once you begin mixing your own glazes and see how easy it is and how much money can be saved, buying pre-mixed glazes becomes a thing of the past. However, it is also true that many people continue to purchase 'special effect' glazes for occasional use or for certain dramatic effects they find difficult to achieve in their own mixes.

There are many ways to apply a glaze, from dipping and pouring to brushing and spraying. These methods are detailed in Chapter 7.

Step 5. Find another clean bucket (it doesn't need to be dry) and fit the sieve into the top of this second bucket. Gradually dump the thick glaze through the sieve, adding some water as you go if you need to in order to get the thickest parts to keep moving, but don't add more than is necessary to get it through the sieve **(3)**.

Put on your gloves and work the glaze through the sieve. You can also use a rubber spatula or a stiff paint-brush to persuade the lumpy glaze through the mesh.

Step 6. Pass the glaze back through the sieve a second time, and then finish adding the right amount of water to the nearly finished glaze. The glaze should be like heavy cream, and 'come to a

gentle stop' once stirred. If after stirring the swirling glaze stops abruptly, add more water. If it swirls on and on and only very gradually stops, then you have probably added too much water. Many potters test their glaze by dipping their finger in it to see how well it coats. You can avoid unnecessary skin contact with your glaze by performing the same test using a dry stir stick.

Once you have mixed the glaze, used it on a piece, and decided that it is the right consistency, you can take some of the guesswork out of mixing future batches by weighing a reproducible volume of the stirred glaze. Find a cup and make a mark on it. Fill the cup to this line with the glaze and weigh it. Next time you mix the glaze do this same measurement and

Correcting glaze-settling problems

There is simply nothing worse than arriving at the studio ready to do some serious glazing, only to be confounded at the outset by a glaze that simply refuses to get stirred up – no matter how long you stir, a hardened layer at the bottom will not budge. Hours can be wasted in attempts to get this layer to mix, only for it to resettle in a matter of minutes when not in use. How can this problem be alleviated?

There are a few materials that tend to settle out of a glaze very quickly, resulting in a glaze that is difficult if not impossible to stir up. The worst offenders are silica, dolomite, any frit, whiting and alumina. Reducing the amounts of these materials in a glaze can help. Using glaze-formulation software can help you choose alternative materials while still making essentially the same glaze. Otherwise, you can add other materials to your glaze to help flocculate it, which means to create little aggregations or 'tufts' of particles that can be suspended in water more easily and do not settle in a hard pancake at the bottom.

The best all-round material that can be added to prevent hard settling is bentonite. Try adding 1–3% (as a percentage of the total **dry** weight of the other materials) to a glaze. Unfortunately, bentonite is nearly

Table 4: Materials that help prevent hard settling of a glaze

Ash	Most ashes tend to have small amounts of soluble alkali metals present. Examples include wood ash, pearl ash and bone ash. Use 1–5% by dry weight of other materials.
Bentonite	Not really a gum, but tends to act like one as its colloidal nature seems to thicken the water. Add 1–5% as a powder when mixing a glaze. Bentonite is simply a clay with very, very fine particles.
Borax	A soluble source of boron and sodium. Usually used in amounts below 1% of the total dry weight of the other materials. Added to the glaze after it is mixed with water. Works by changing the ionic composition of the mixture.
CMC powdered gum	Sodium carboxymethylcellulose, an organic cellulose gum. Mix 1 to 2 tablespoons per 4.5l (1.2 US gal.) of warm water and let stand for 24 hours. Pour into the glaze during the wet mixing process OR do the following: add 50g (1.8oz) of the dry gum to one litre of very hot water in a blender. Blend this mixture very well, allow it to stand for a day, and then blend again. This gum works by thickening the water portion of the mix. This will tend to mould after awhile so keep your glaze in a refrigerator or just use it quickly.
Darvan 7	A soluble polyelectrolyte. Used in small amounts below 1% of total volume. Changes the ionic composition of the mix.
Darvan 811	Similar to Darvan 7. Slightly different mechanism for creating ions. Follow manufacturer's recommendation for usage.
Epsom salt	Epsom salt is normally easy to find for sale at a chemist or drug store, in the bath section. It is used as a water softener and contains soluble magnesium sulphate. Epsom salts change the ionic composition of mixed glaze. Use in small amounts, about ½ to 1 tablespoon per 4.5l (1.2 US gal.).
Flocs	Flocs is a trade name for a material sold as a glaze suspender. It is completely organic and burns off during the firing, indicating it has a gum component similar to CMC. It also tends to crystallise if left for long periods and allowed to cool, indicating it has a soluble component. Use 1 teaspoon per 22.5l (6 US gal.) of mixed glaze.
Soda ash	Sodium carbonate – soluble. Changes the ionic composition and pH of the mixed glaze. Try in amounts less than 1% by dry weight of ingredients.
Sodium silicate	Water-soluble solution of sodium oxide (soda) and silica oxide (silica). If too much is added will have the effect of causing the glaze to resettle. Try using 1 teaspoon per 4.5l. (1.2 US gal.) of water. Sodium silicate changes the ionic composition of the mix; also known as water glass.
Table salt	Soluble sodium chloride. Changes ionic composition of mix. Use in small amounts, about ½ to 1 tablespoon per 4.5l (1.2 US gal.).
Veegum CER	A mixture of Veegum T and CMC. It is sold as a glaze hardener (meaning, your glaze will be tougher when you are loading it in the kiln), but also helps to suspend glazes. Add 1–1.5% based on the dry weight formula. Can disperse in water or be added directly to dry mix. Works at least in part by adding a gum to the water, thereby thickening it. Veegum, despite the name, is actually a fine-particled volcanic clay similar to bentonite.
Veegum T	A magnesium aluminium silicate. Add 0.5–1.5% by weight of dry ingredients to water and then to mixed glaze. A gum that thickens the water.

impossible to add to a glaze that is already wet; it has to be blended in with the other dry materials when the glaze is first mixed. You can always mix up a second batch of the glaze with the bentonite and add it to the first to try and help an existing settling problem.

Other materials that can help with settling issues are listed in the table opposite. Use caution when adding any of these materials to a glaze, as too much might change the glaze and ruin it. Additionally, any of the soluble materials listed can cause skin irritation or a rash if in contact with skin for more than a short period. Wear rubber gloves, wash after using glazes, and wear eye protection when mixing. Some of the gums listed will mould after a few weeks, so keep glazes containing these gums cold or use them quickly.

DISPOSING OF WASTE GLAZES

What to do with all those glaze tests that just did not work, or all those old cups of now unlabelled glazes? Can they just be dumped down the drain? The most responsible answer is NO! Glazes that have no colourants and no hazardous flux oxides in them (barium and lead are the most common) can be put down the drain, as the remaining materials are harmless to the environment. All other glazes should be dealt with more carefully. Read the health and safety section (p.p.155–6) for ideas on how to safely dispose of unwanted glazes.

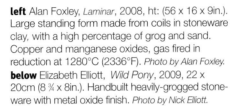

left Alan Foxley, *Laminar*, 2008, ht: (56 x 16 x 9in.). Large standing form made from coils in stoneware clay, with a high percentage of grog and sand. Copper and manganese oxides, gas fired in reduction at 1280°C (2336°F). *Photo by Alan Foxley.*
below Elizabeth Elliott, *Wild Pony*, 2009, 22 x 20cm (8 ¾ x 8in.). Handbuilt heavily-grogged stoneware with metal oxide finish. *Photo by Nick Elliott.*

7

DECORATING TECHNIQUES

Decorating clay objects can be a complicated affair or a very simple task. Bare clay can be one of the most satisfying surfaces to look at (see image below).

Most objects to be used with food are covered with glaze to make clean-up easier. For some, the ceramic surface is another kind of canvas to which they can add their design work. Depending on which aspect of ceramic art you are drawn to (or which of your pieces tends to be most marketable), either making the objects or decorating them can evolve into the single main aspect of how you work. For those that decorate, the information below will help guide you through some of the main areas of decorating.

GLAZING

Glazing is probably the most common way of decorating a piece of pottery. It is truly one of the most distinguishing qualities of finished clay art: a glass-coated ceramic object. Some ceramic pieces can be made to look like other forms of art, such as carved wood or painted canvas, but it is very difficult for the reverse to be true, as pieces with a glassy, durable coating really stand out.

When it comes to making a piece of glazed ceramic work look good when finished, the importance of how a glaze was applied cannot be overstated. A good glaze on a great piece when poorly applied can easily ruin everything. Practice makes perfect, so be sure to try your techniques several times before deciding whether they are right for you.

Most people make big messes the first time they are trying a new application technique; try not to be put off! Study the problem and try to come up with a solution: a better way of supporting the piece; different equipment or tools that you could use; or more time taken to get the desired effect. Be meticulous in your efforts to achieve your goals, and practise your methods as often as possible.

Most potters apply glazes to pieces that have been fired once already (bisque-fired). A smaller number apply their glazes to pieces that are still damp and will be 'single-fired' when dry. Sculptors do what they like, applying glazes when the pieces are wet, damp, dry, bisque-fired or even after they are glaze-fired, to achieve multiple firing effects. Experiment! Try some new things and see what results you get.

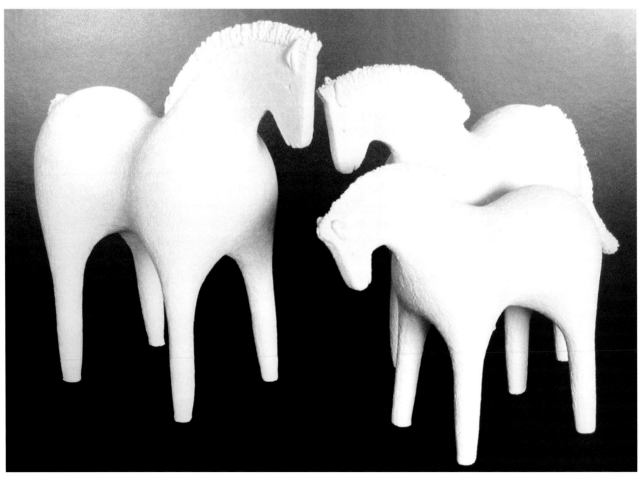

Elizabeth Elliott, *Prezwalski's Horse*, 2006, 16 x 21cm (8¼ x 6 ¼in.). Hand-formed from grogged white stoneware. Unglazed. *Photo by Nick Elliott.*

General glazing guidelines

There are several guidelines to follow no matter which technique you are using. Most glazes settle quickly and must therefore be stirred immediately before use and regularly during use (every few minutes is best) to ensure the glaze will do what it is supposed to do. Some ingredients settle faster than others, so you might not be getting the whole glaze if you don't stir it on a regular basis.

During a firing, melting glaze will stick to whatever it contacts. Glaze on the bottom of a pot will cause the pot to become permanently affixed to your glaze shelf! Too much glaze will result in a runny mess that will also stick a pot to the kiln shelf (see image, right).

Glaze pooling around the bottom of a pot.

Be careful not to overdo it. If you are unsure, put your pieces on sand in the kiln or on pieces of unglazed pottery to catch any runs, so as not to damage your kiln.

Glaze mistakes made during application can usually be washed off with water (at least if your piece has been bisque-fired initially) and a sponge, but after washing, a wet pot will not absorb glaze easily and therefore must be allowed to dry before being re-glazed (a matter of hours or even days).

Do not forget that bare clay can be beautiful! Vitrified clay can be lovely to look at and is as tough and durable as glass, so food contact with stoneware clays is perfectly acceptable. Some people use unglazed earthenware for food as well. However, the more porous nature of earthenware will mean it absorbs food particles, oils and spices. This can either be a problem or an opportunity, depending on your perspective.

Siglinda Scarpa, *Fishpot* and other vessels, 2010, 46 x 31 x 23cm (18 x 12 x 9in.). Unglazed cooking pot fired to cone 7. *Photo by Jennifer A. Siegel.*

BASIC METHODS OF GLAZE APPLICATION:
brushing, dipping, pouring and spraying

Brushing is usually the most straightforward of all glazing techniques, as most people have had experience with painting at some point in their lives. Glazes, however, tend to be fairly unforgiving as brushstrokes will often show in the finished glaze. It can be tedious to brush a glaze all over a big pot, especially a bisque-fired pot that quickly absorbs the moisture from the glaze. To help you in this task, try making large unhindered movements with a big sopping-wet brush. It's OK if you miss a few places, as the negative spaces left behind can add interest to the pot. It is difficult to achieve fine detail with glazes as they tend to melt and bleed into one another. Most fine detail is achieved with underglaze colours that don't melt, or by applying a colourant such as a stain or enamel on top of a glaze, sometimes after the glaze firing. Since glazes tend to want to flow, be loose with your movements and go with the flow! Try different-shaped brushes, especially soft 'mop head' brushes or long trailing liner or calligraphy brushes. Bamboo ones can work especially well.

Dipping is probably the most common way of applying a glaze. It is a fast technique that avoids the problems of brushstrokes showing up, but does pose other difficulties. First, you must have mixed up enough glaze in a large-enough container to allow your piece to be dipped. Second, you have to be physically able to pick up your piece (not all pieces are easy to move!). Third, there must be no glaze on the bottom of the piece when it goes into the kiln or it will stick to the kiln shelf. Dipping usually means the bottom will get glaze on it, so you will have to wipe it off at some point before firing. Fourth, what about

Applying a glaze with a large brush.

Dipping a pot into a glaze using tongs.

Wiping glaze off the bottom of a dipped pot.

Glaze applied too thick will sometimes crack. This glaze will need to be washed off and reapplied.

your hands? You will have to hold onto the piece in some way when it is dipped, and finger marks on the rim of your bowl might not be the look you are trying to achieve. And fifth, what if your piece fills up with glaze when dipped? How do you get it out? Read on to find out!

The simplest way to dip is to use glaze tongs (see opposite), which are available from most supply stores. These will only work with bisque-fired pieces as they pinch the pot tightly between their teeth. Use the tongs to fully submerge the piece in the glaze, and count the seconds. Most glazes mixed to the right consistency will coat a bisque-fired pot well in 3–5 seconds of contact. When you pull the piece out of the glaze, invert it and dump out any extra glaze. Keep the piece inverted for 5–10 seconds to let the excess glaze drip off the top. This will also have the benefit of reducing the amount of glaze near the bottom of the pot, reducing the likelihood of the glaze running and sticking to the kiln. While it is inverted, if possible use a damp sponge and water to wipe the bottom clear of glaze.

It is very important to remember to wipe the bottom, and then starting from the base remove the glaze to between 0.5 and 1cm (about 3⁄8in.) up the sides as well, again to reduce the chances of the piece sticking to the kiln shelf. A little colourant-haze left behind on the bottom is OK, but try to get all the glaze drips out of any grooves or cracks.

The marks left by the tongs can usually be ignored as they will blend out during the firing, but a few rubs with a finger or a dab with a brush can help as well.

The amount of glaze on a pot applied by dipping can be measured in the number of seconds of contact. If a whole pot is dipped for 5 seconds in one glaze, and then dipped again for 5 more seconds in a second glaze, then that is 10 seconds of glaze on the pot. Too much glaze on a pot will result in a runny disaster in the kiln, so be aware of how much you have applied! Most pots will run too much if they have more than about 6–7 seconds of glaze on an exterior vertical surface (interiors, of course, are a different matter, and more glaze can typically be applied inside than out). Also, very thick glaze applications tend to form cracks on the surface as they dry, which then result in patches of unglazed areas on the finished pot (see photo on p.97).

Pouring a glaze on a piece is really just a localised dipping method. If the stream of glaze being poured over a piece continues for about 5 seconds, then that area of glaze will have a very similar look to a piece that has been dipped for 5 seconds. Try pouring different patterns and shapes onto your piece, regarding areas that you miss as negative space. You don't need to cover the whole piece with glaze! The unglazed clay is there as an additional colour for you to take advantage of and show off.

There are few things to keep in mind when pouring: pour from bottom to top, or sideways, but not top to bottom if it can be helped. This will reduce the build-up of excess glaze near the bottom where it might run and stick the pot to the kiln. Pouring a glaze into the interior of a piece, such as a mug, then dumping it out is a clever way of getting just the one glaze colour on the inside of a piece. If you then invert it, and plunge it carefully into a different glaze, the air pocket formed on the inside will allow you to have a different colour on the inside than the outside. Again, be sure to wipe the bottom of your piece free of glaze before firing.

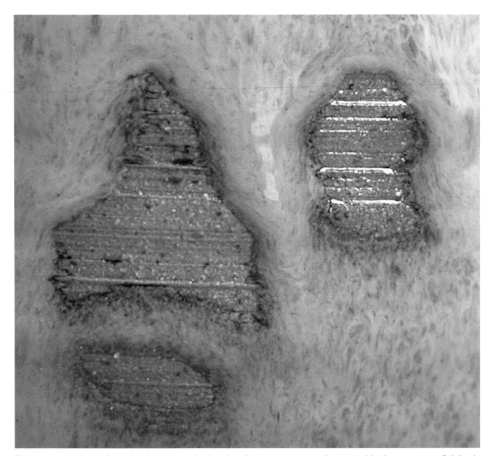

If not corrected, cracks or bad coverage in the dry glaze can go on to become blank areas on a finished piece after firing.However, areas of unglazed pot can look great if left deliberately for decoration.

Applying a glaze by pouring.

Spraying a glaze can be accomplished in several ways. The most expensive way is to have a spray booth, an air compressor and a variety of air brushes at your disposal. If you're on a budget, it is possible to use sprayers that are powered by your breath, which are sold by many suppliers. Alternatively, you can use an air brush outdoors without a spray booth, though there are some environmental considerations that should be taken into account before releasing raw glaze chemicals into your back garden – basically, it's not a good idea, so only do it if you can somehow collect the overspray and recycle or dispose of it properly. Spray bottles do not work well with glazes, as the particles in the glaze tend to clog them up, but some of the colourants by themselves, mixed with water, can be used this way when sprayed on top of a glaze that has already been applied. Try spraying some dark colourants over a light-coloured glaze and see what effects you get, but bear in mind that too much of a colourant on a surface meant for food may render the piece hazardous.

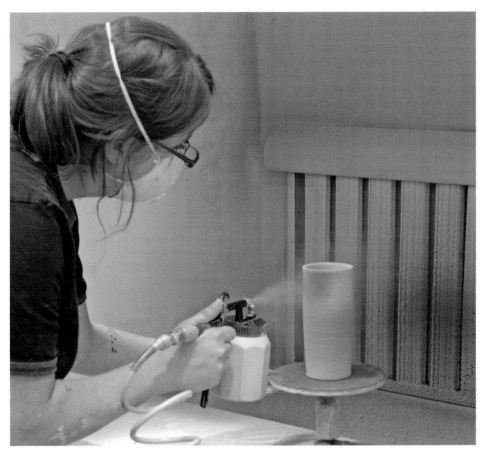

Applying glaze in a spray booth.

Lyn Morrow, *Bowl,* 2008, 55 x 18cm (22 x 7 in.). Thrown porcelain bowl with chattered texture applied on the wheel. Chattered texture is created using a flexible carving tool, held at an angle on the pot while it turns on the wheel once the piece is leatherhard, it drags along the surface and bounces rapidly creating a ridged pattern. Sprayed glaze application, reduction fired to cone 11.
Photo by Catherine Whitten.

Additional glaze application techniques

There are about as many ways to apply a glaze to a piece as there are ceramic artists in the world. Below is a list of some techniques to try with a brief description of each. Give several a try and soon new ideas will come to you that might work well with the pieces you make.

Dripping: Move your piece underneath a drip or a stream of glaze coming out of a hole in a suspended container (catch the excess in a bucket below).

Sponging: Use sponges with various textures and shapes to create interesting effects.

Trailing/basting: Use a slip-trailing bottle (available from ceramic suppliers) or some other squeezable bottle with a narrow-pointed tip (hair-dye application bottles work well), or use a turkey baster, to apply lines to your piece. These lines show up best when not on top of another glaze, where they tend to bleed in and disappear.

Finger swipes: After dipping or pouring, while the glaze is still wet, drag your fingers through the glaze to make designs.

Wax resist: Various kinds of wax can be used, but an emulsion in water purchased from a ceramic supplier is usually easiest. Paint this onto your

Opposite page
above Tom Gray, *Dragonfly Bowl*, 2009, 33 x 9cm (13 x 3.5in.). Wheel-thrown, decorated with glaze and slip-trailing, with the slip being made from locally dug clay. *Photo by the artist.*

below Andy Phillips, *Stoneware Oven Dish*, 2008, 24 x 8cm (9½ x 3in.). Thrown dish with extruded handles. Blue base glaze followed by brushed wax-resist decoration, then dipped in second glaze. Fired to cone 6 in an electric kiln. *Photo by the artist.*

right Joe Cole, *Pitcher with Fish Decoration*, 2007, ht: 38cm (15 in.). Wheel-thrown and wood-fired. An example of finger wipes in a wet glaze. *Photo by Tim Ayers.*

piece before glazing, or try painting over an already applied glaze before dipping a second time.

Scratching: Use a sharp object to scratch off some glaze. This is especially effective when working with still soft clay meant for a single firing.

DECORATING WITH COLOURED LIQUID CLAYS
(underglazes, slips, terra sigillata and engobes)

Underglazes, slips, terra sigillata and engobes are really just four terms for the same thing: coloured liquid clay. Whatever they are called, they can all be used in similar ways.

Coloured clays are very versatile, and time should be spent experimenting with how they work and what they can do before you commit to a single technique. Most often these materials are applied in the same ways as glazes: by dipping, pouring, brushing or spraying, but usually at the leatherhard stage instead of after bisquing. Once the coloured clays have been applied, the pieces can be bisque-fired to 'set' the decoration, and then glazed. Thick opaque glazes will usually completely hide whatever is underneath them, while leaving the pieces unglazed will show off the clay decoration to its maximum,

and coloured translucent glazes will lend depth to the decoration. Many coloured clays will peel and fall off if applied directly to bisque ware although liquid gums can be added to help them adhere; check with your supplier for the right one to purchase. Many coloured clays will work just fine on top of glazes (despite the name 'underglaze') and can be applied after the glazes dry.

Another way of working with coloured clays is to cover a leather-hard piece with a con-trasting colour, and then to carve through the applied colour to create the deco-ration (as in this bowl, right). Slips, like glazes, can be trailed using a slip trailing bottle or baster (see pp.100-101).

An easy recipe to use to make a general-pur-pose underglaze can be found in the section on recipes at the end of the book. Colourants can be added to it, but care must be taken when applying coloured clays to surfaces intended to be used with food, as underglazes do not bind colourants as well as glazes, and leaching of hazardous materials into food can occur.

Terra sigillata is a more specialised slip or under-glaze. It is a very fine-particled slip that can be burnished with a cloth or smooth stone after application to a leatherhard or dry piece. Getting a real shine from terra sigillata takes a lot of work and is time-consuming, but can give lovely results. Burnishing tends to be done as an alternative to glazing (not as well as), as the glaze can ruin the shine, as can firing it above low earthenware temperatures.

opposite, top left Ronan Peterson, *Hornet's Nest Cruet Set*, 2008, 25.5 x 35.5 x 35.5cm (10 x 14 x 14in.). Oxidation-fired earthenware. An example of the kind of effects that can be achieved using terra sigillata for decoration. *Photo by Tom Mills Photography.*

left Nichola Theakston, *Stalking Cheetah*, 2007–08, 52 x 27cm (20½ x 10½in.). Decorated with coloured slips, and wax and pigment patina applied after firing. Once fired to 1170°C (2138°F). *Photo by the artist.*

above Leanne Pizio, *Treemakers Bowl*, 2009, 31 x 11.5cm (12 x 4⅛in.). Cone 6 white stoneware, brushed black slip with carved sgraffito decoration. *Photo by William Pizio.*

DECORATING WITH LUSTRES AND ENAMELS
(china paints and on-glazes)

Many people believe that once a piece has been glaze-fired, it is done. Not so! More colours and decorations can be added on top of a glaze, and then the piece can be fired again (and again!). An oil-based medium is frequently used to get more material to adhere to a potentially glossy, vitrified surface. Metallic lustres suspend bright metals including gold and silver in an oily liquid that can be easily brushed onto the surface of a glaze. Enamels, also known as china paints and on-glazes, work in the same way, but the colour choice is much larger. The firing temperatures for these materials are very low, usually around cone 018, which succeeds in getting the oily medium to burn off, leaving just the decoration behind on the surface. As the colourants left behind on the surface of a glaze are not very durable, the food safety issues surrounding the use of these on functional ware are contentious at best, despite the fact that these materials have been used on dishware for many years. These products can be bought ready-made from suppliers.

DECORATING WITH (MAIOLICA) STAINS

Stains are very simple: colourants – sometimes mixed with a frit – and water. Not to be confused with mason stains (from which they are often made), they can also be made from raw colourants such as cobalt and copper. They can be used in a variety of ways, including as a wash on wet, dry or bisqued pieces, or they can be applied on top of wet or dry underglazes or glazes. With no ability to melt or fuse on their own, the only way to get them to stick to the piece they are applied to is to take advantage of any melting, fusing or vitrifying occurring around them. Food safety is a big concern with stains, as colourants pose the biggest health hazards, so it is not a good idea to apply them carelessly to pieces intended to be used with food.

left Julia Roxburgh, *Mixed Pattern Teapot with Legs*, 2006, ht: 28cm (11 in.). White earthenware with slip-trailing, underglazes and gold lustre. Fired four times: bisque, underglaze, glaze, lustre. *Photo by David Lawson.*

opposite
above right Doug Dotson, *Bottle*, 2009, 23 x 23 x 23cm (9 x 9 x 9in.). Thrown and altered stoneware, fired to cone 10 in a soda firing. *Photo by the artist.*
below right The easy to find MSDS book in the clay studio.

Maiolica stains

Many people are familiar with ceramic stains as used on maiolica (also known as majolica, delftware, Hispano-Moresque ware, faience and English delftware): bright colours brushed onto a milky-white background. This decorating technique has been used for hundreds of years, and was developed by European potters attempting to make Chinese porcelain-like pieces long before they had the materials or the knowhow to do so. The white tin-based low-temperature glaze was applied to earthenware pieces, and then the stains were painstakingly painted on. The slightest touch would disturb the stains, so extreme caution had to be used while applying subsequent details. Many tiles, pots and sculptures are still made this way today. (See the image of the *Elizabeth Mary Devon Bowl*, p.111).

How to make a maiolica stain

To make a maiolica stain, simply mix equal amounts of a mason stain and ferro frit 3195, add water and stir to make a very thin, watery mix. Apply this over a dry maiolica glaze with a brush (see glaze recipe on p.157). If it is dry and crusty after firing, you need to add more frit to the next one, and if it bleeds too much, add more colourant and water instead.

ALTERNATIVE DECORATING METHODS: salt, soda and fly ash

If you are lucky enough to have a salt-, soda- or wood-fired kiln for your use, you can actually glaze your work while it is being fired! See Chapter 10 on firing kilns for more information on these hands-off decorating techniques.

SAFETY WHILE DECORATING

It is advisable to have on hand MSDS (Material Safety Data Sheets) for all the materials you use in your studio. These can be requested from your ceramic supplier. MSDS sheets give you information on the hazards posed by the chemicals you are using, telling you in what way they are hazardous (respiration versus contact) and in what amounts. They also provide some information on what to do in case you come in contact with a material in a dangerous way.

Keep in mind that even if you are careful to source materials from reputable suppliers and the materials indicate that they are non-toxic, no one can guarantee that the combinations used on your pieces fired in your particular way will not cause dangerous fumes to be emitted during a firing or result in a non-food-safe product.

Remember also that labels indicating the level of safety of a ceramic material can be misleading. Some refer to the safety of a material post-firing, not the safety of the material in its raw form. This is especially true for commercial glazes and underglazes. Many that are labelled 'non-toxic' are in fact toxic in their pre-firing liquid forms and only become non-toxic if fired correctly! Be sure to read the fine print on the containers.

To be safe, always treat raw materials and firing kilns as unsafe industrial processes. See the health and safety section at the end of the book for more safety information.

8

Correcting Glaze Faults

GLAZE DETECTIVE WORK:
determining when a problem occurred

Misbehaving glazes! Almost nothing is more frustrating. All the work required to prepare the piece, all the time spent firing, and then ... disaster! All clay artists who work with glazes have experienced a time or two when their glazes have gone awry. After a few years, most develop an elusive skill: the ability to deduce from various clues the when, where and how of glaze misadventures.

It is often quite tricky to determine just when a glaze problem occurred and exactly what should be done to keep it from happening again. As often as not, there will be more than one way to fix a given problem, although one solution is usually a lot easier than another. In this chapter a variety of possible problems are listed along with some ideas for fixing them. And, of course, becoming adept at determining how to address the particular problems you are having will become easier with practice.

There are at least four different points along the way to firing a glazed piece of pottery where a problem can arise. These are: during the formulation of the glaze recipe, when mixing the glaze, when applying the glaze, and during firing. At any one of these points, a potentially good glaze can be rendered problematic. Of course, if you are using a store-bought glaze, your prospects for resolving problems with that glaze will be severely limited as you won't know the ingredients that went into it. Your best bet might be to abandon the problem glaze and purchase something else. Or, better yet, decide to mix your own glazes, over time developing a range that works well for you.

Sometimes it's better to use little or no glaze on your piece. Dennis Kilgallon, *River God*, 2005, 66 x 50 x 14cm (26.5 x 19.5 x 5.5 in.). Press moulded from original cast in plaster, dusted with whiting when dry and once-fired to 1300°C (2372°F). *Photo by the artist.*

PROBLEMS ARISING FROM THE RECIPE

Many glaze success stories and disasters begin and end with the recipe. Small changes in the amount of an ingredient can make a huge difference in the way a glaze behaves. Finding the right recipe quickly without spending hours and hours testing and retesting is a good goal to have, but can be difficult to achieve. If a glaze recipe is simply not good, results with that glaze will be poor no matter what small incremental changes you try. About the only way to tell if a recipe is good without making it and firing it is to run it through glaze-formulation software and analyse the makeup. People skilled in this technique save themselves days of waiting for tests to come out of kilns. How to do this is covered in Chapter 9.

Generally, however, good glazes contain a mixture of enough raw materials to create a viable finished glaze. A good glaze recipe will contain the right ingredients to ensure that the glaze 'behaves' in the bucket, is easy to apply, will fire correctly and (above all) will look good. How a glaze behaves before firing will not be made evident through studying results provided by glaze-formulation software, but only through trial and error and through experience.

Below is a general list of the five different materials nearly all glazes need to function well:

Clay (usually kaolin or ball clay)
Feldspar and/or **frit**
Silica
A second source of flux oxides (e.g. whiting, dolomite, wollastonite, gerstley borate or others)
Colourants and/or **opacifiers** (if the glaze is not meant to be clear). Brief descriptions of these materials were given in Chapter 5.

If you find a glaze recipe with only two

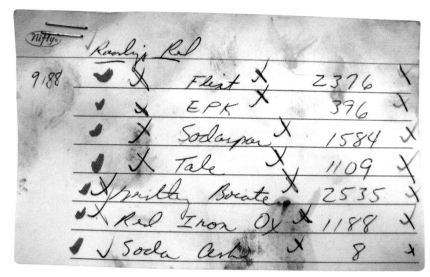

An old, messy glaze recipe card that should be replaced by one that is easier to read and interpret, which will reduce the likelihood of errors during mixing. *Photo by Jennifer A. Siegel.*

ingredients, the chances are it will not work well. Recipes with eight or more ingredients also start to look dubious. Nearly all successful glazes have between five and eight.

PROBLEMS ARISING FROM MIXING THE GLAZE

It is easy enough when mixing a glaze to be in a hurry and simply skip the addition of one ingredient. Work towards having good, clear recipes to follow. Check off each ingredient as you add it, and look back on your work as you progress to see that you have not been taking the wrong material out of the wrong bucket. Make sure you know how to use your scale accurately and how to 'tare' the scale so that you are not accidentally including the weight of the container on the scale as well as the material.

Be sure to dry-mix the ingredients before adding water, and be sure to sieve the ingredients at least twice to ensure a complete and thorough mix. Follow carefully the directions given in Chapter 6 (see pp.88–9) on mixing glazes.

There are often invisible soluble ingredients contained in the water of a glaze, so try not to go the route of adding too much water and then scooping off the excess once the glaze has settled, as you may be inadvertently removing these dissolved materials. If the glaze settles too quickly or too compactly, try using another ingredient to keep the material in suspension for longer, as this will help with application (see p.90 for further details).

PROBLEMS ARISING DURING APPLICATION

By far the most common problem that occurs to people when applying glazes is over-application. Many people are looking for dynamic glaze results with tantalising swirls and dazzling mixtures of colour. While thicker applications of glaze can produce these sorts of results, the amount of good work that gets destroyed by runny glazes is huge. Pay attention to glaze thickness. If it appears to be too thick, wash it off, dry out the pot and start again. Try to make sure that the thickest glaze areas end up as far from the kiln shelf as possible, i.e. near the top or on the insides of the piece.

The flip side of the thickness problem occurs when glazes are under-applied. This can happen for a variety of reasons: dipping or spraying too quickly, having a pot that is wet before applying a glaze, or not stirring the glaze immediately before application. These pieces tend to look shabby and a bit uninspiring after firing.

A wide array of other small issues can arise from failure to pay attention to details while applying a glaze. Fingerprints from wax or water can keep glaze from adhering well; dust in or on the piece can do the same; not smoothing rough or uneven glaze can result in surface faults; knocking or chipping off bits of glaze prior to loading can ruin a good piece. Take time to look at each piece carefully after glazing. If it does not look good going into the kiln, the chances are it will not look good coming out of it.

Most application problems fall into two categories: those that can be fixed with a little touching up and those that require completely starting over. It is important to remember that in the kiln the glaze will melt and move around a little bit, so small problem areas may just smooth over and go away. Fixing little problems can usually be handled by touching up with a brush, rubbing and smoothing with a fingertip, or wiping off and reapplying with a brush. All of these methods work well for pieces that have been bisque-fired first. With single-fired pieces, allow the pot to dry completely before touching up, as a freshly glazed damp pot can become very unstable and weak.

If the glazing has really gone badly, and needs to be completely removed, with a bisque-fired pot this can be accomplished by washing the pot in a bucket of water and scrubbing with a sponge. Allow the pot to dry completely before reapplying glaze. This may take several days. In a bucket try to collect the glaze you wash off pots and dispose of it safely rather than allowing glaze chemicals to go down the drain, as these pose an environmental hazard (see health and safety, pp.155–6).

above This glaze has been applied too thickly, and has also not been wiped off the bottom prior to firing. During the firing, the glaze has melted and stuck to the shelf. *Photo by Jennifer A. Siegel.*

top This pot clearly has some glaze application issues that might best be remedied by washing all the glaze off and starting over. If fired, the fingerprints and cracked glaze will detract from the finish, and the thick glaze will most likely run and stick to the kiln shelf. *Photo by Jennifer A. Siegel.*

above The same pot after firing shows the results of sloppy glaze application. *Photo by Jennifer A. Siegel.*

PROBLEMS DURING THE FIRING

Knowing how to get the best out of your glazes through proper firing is a huge and complex area of study. It can take artists years to get their kiln-firing schedules the way that works best for them, so don't forget the importance of paying attention to this part of the process. Many artists spend time changing glazes or clays or materials in their attempts to solve a problem, but never bother to study their firing schedules. A small adjustment in the firing schedule can make a big difference in the appearance and performance of a glaze.

More information on firing schedules will be provided in Chapter 10. Here are a few ideas to pay attention to when looking to make positive changes to your schedule.

Underfiring a glaze can result in dry, crusty glazes or colours that are not mature. Try firing the glaze to the next highest cone value and see if things improve. Conversely, overfired glazes can run excessively and even boil into a glass 'foam'. Try reducing the temperature of the firing by a cone.

Great results can come from taking extreme care when decorating your work. Ronan Peterson, *Stump Jar (Lightning Bug),* 2008, 20 x 15 x 15cm (8 x 6 x 6 in.). Oxidation-fired earthenware. *Photo by Fancy Rondo Prod.*

The materials making up your clay body and your glaze undergo a variety of transformations during a firing. As mentioned in Chapter 4, the first thing to happen is that moisture will be driven off, and then, after that, carbon will burn off. Adequate time needs to be allowed for these processes to occur, so that these materials can make their way out from the clay body and through the glaze.

More fumes and gases are driven off at high temperatures, too. If a glaze is fired too fast, these escaping gases will show up as problems such as pinholes or bubbles. If your pieces exhibit these problems, slow down your firing somewhat. Add another hour to the initial drying-out period, and add an hour near the top temperatures to allow for a 'soaking' of heat, with the goal that the additional time will allow gases to escape and the glaze to smooth out.

Soaking in a kiln can lead to excessive running, so watch your results and adjust accordingly. For more ideas take a look at the firing-schedule graphs at the end of the book (see p.155).

HAPPY ACCIDENTS

As much as many of us would like to think we are in control of what is happening with our work, the reality is that we are very much unable to control a lot of what happens. The materials we buy might be dug from a different vein of ore in the ground; the water we use to mix the glaze with might change its chemistry; the elements in our kiln weaken gradually over time; and the wood we burn in our kilns is never the same from one tree to the next. Ultimately, with ceramics, there is inevitably an element of chance in every piece we make. As much as we would sometimes like there to be a simple answer as to why something goes wrong, often there is none. Look to these moments when things go wrong for inspiration, as sometimes the glaze that has run onto our kiln shelf is simply breathtaking, or the fragments of a piece that exploded are simply gorgeous. See if you can find and use some good aspect of a problem to your future advantage. A lot of the wonderful pieces that you see at shows and in shops have evolved from a history of disaster!

Getting your glaze to turn out just right can take years of practice. Detail of Eck and Zeke McCanless's *Elizabeth Mary Devon Bowl,* 2006–09. *Photo by Misty Donathan.*

9
GLAZE FORMULATION

WHY DO GLAZE FORMULATION (and what is it)?

Artistry and science are too often like oil and water: sometimes they just do not want to get mixed up together. But there are many art students who excel at science, and many scientists who rely on their creativity to carry out their tests. Thankfully, art and science have been mixing successfully recently in a new way for ceramic artists. The development of relatively simple-to-use and affordable glaze-formulation software has brought this science of working with ceramic materials within everyone's reach.

The relevant software, which is sold by several companies, can do a variety of things, but the core value they all share is the ability to look at raw glaze materials and translate them into the materials – oxides – that are found in the fired glazes. As has been discussed in previous chapters of this book, glaze and glass are made up of oxides. They are not made up of clays, feldspars or frits. While these were the raw materials that went into the kiln, the glaze that formed from them during the firing is a completely different substance, with different properties and structure. Until the creation of glaze software, very, very few artists attempted to study glaze formulation at the oxide level, as the process involved doing very long, drawn-out computations on paper. But what used to take days to sort out now takes seconds.

Traditionally, all artists have relied on the results of their firings acting as tests of their glazes, but those that now use the glaze software can reduce the amount of trial and error in their test glazes by at least half. While the initial cost of the software and the time it takes to get used to it can at first seem untenable, within a short space of time artists seeking to develop and enhance their glaze repertoire normally find themselves saving hundreds of hours and lots of money.

THE TRADITIONAL METHOD: Line blending

The traditional, and still common, way of formulating a glaze or attempting to fix a problematic glaze is to do a series of line blends, or incremental educated guesses. This process takes time, plenty of test tiles, and a good understanding of the oxides that make up the raw materials being used and what the oxides derived from them do in the glaze. The artist uses tables to sort out which oxides are present of the raw materials, and then makes an educated guess as to which raw material should be changed to make the desired change in the fired glaze. There is always some doubt as to the exact amount by which the raw ingredient should be changed, so incremental changes are made to the glaze, the glaze mixed and applied to test tiles, and then the test tiles fired and the results studied. From the results, further tests can be calculated and performed to advance the process, until satisfactory results are achieved.

For example, if the recipe to be used was the following:

Glaze recipe 9.1 cone 6

Dolomite	25.3
Spodumene	21.3
Frit 3134	6.8
Ball clay	23.3
Silica	23.3

The above glaze recipe will make a glaze at cone 6. Without colourants it is a semi-transparent, semi-gloss, milky-white glaze. If you want to make this glaze into a cone 10 glaze using line blending, you will first need to obtain some information about the chemistry of your raw materials. A lot of information is available online: try www.digitalfire.com to start with. Also, many books offer good information on glaze material chemistry. A classic one is Daniel Rhodes's *Clay and Glazes for the Potter* (no relation to this author!).

Testing glazes in the glaze room of a ceramic department at college. *Photo by the artist.*

Glaze recipe 9.1 fired to cone 6. *Photo by Jennifer A. Siegel.*

Starting with your glaze recipe above, increase the amount of ball clay and silica by 1% for each of the ten tests.

The first test you would make up would therefore be:

Dolomite	25.3
Spodumene	21.3
Frit 3134	6.8
Ball clay	24.3
Silica	24.3

If you did this in grams, your batch size would then be 102 grams. Mix this up thoroughly and carefully, and apply to a test tile.

Next, increase the same two ingredients by 1% again, and apply to your next test tile. Keep on going until the amount of ball clay and silica is 33.3 grams each, and your batch size is 120 grams. Somewhere in this 'line' of tests might be the one that works. Fire all the tiles to cone 10 and see which one works the best, if any. Then, if you see promising results, you can fine-tune them with another line blend, this time isolating just the silica in relationship to the ball clay, or you could try changing another ingredient, such as spodumene (a lithium feldspar), which is also a source of silica oxide and alumina oxide. Using the books and the online resources to learn what each raw material provides in terms of oxides to the fired glaze is the secret to getting good at this method of working.

Another way to work is to use glaze-formulation software. After a fair amount of practice, in just a few minutes you can determine that a recipe likely to work at cone 10 will be:

Glaze recipe 9.2 fired to cone 10. *Photo by Jennifer A. Siegel*

Recipe 9.2, cone 10

Dolomite	20.1
Spodumene	20.1
Frit 3134	5.9
Ball clay	29.4
Silica	24.5

Testing this result will still take time, and it may not work just right the first time, so it would still be a good idea to do a few tests on either side (using the traditional line-blending method) of these values to see if the results can be improved.

Obviously, making changes to a glaze can require a lot of time and effort. Reading the following section about how to do glaze formulation can help to take some of the guesswork out of the line-blending process. You will still have to do several test tiles to work out the very best glaze, so knowing how to do line-blending is an indispensible tool. Formulating glazes using the software can speed up the process somewhat, and has generally made the development of new glazes much easier.

Once you have a few tables with the information about your raw materials in front of you, you can begin to make educated guesses as to which raw materials to increase or decrease to get the results you want. For this example, your best bet would be to increase the amounts of silica oxide and alumina oxide relative to the amounts of fluxes, so that the glaze will 'mature', or melt sufficiently, at the increased cone value. Primarily, ball clay is a good source of alumina and silica oxides (see Chapter 5, p.p.78–9), so increasing the amount of ball clay would be a good starting point. But by how much? And what about the silica that is also listed as an ingredient in the glaze? As you will learn, it is important to keep the same amount of silica oxide relative to alumina oxide. Since the last ingredient in the recipe, silica, is also used to source silica oxide in the fired glaze, we have to increase this ingredient as well as the clay to keep things in balance. Now comes the line blending, so prepare about ten test tiles for the first run-through.

GLAZE FORMULATION: Where to begin

The first step is to purchase and install the software on your computer. Two companies that will allow you to do this via an internet download are detailed in the list of suppliers at the end of this book.

As previously stated, glaze-formulation software has at its core the ability to translate a glaze recipe composed of raw materials directly into the oxides that will compose the fired glaze. Let's look at glaze recipe 9.1 again and the oxides that compose the fired glaze:

Glaze recipe 9.1 cone 6

Dolomite	25.3
(A source of calcium and magnesium oxides)	
Spodumene	21.3
(A feldspar sourcing lithium, silica and alumina oxides)	
Frit 3134	6.8
(A manmade feldspar sourcing calcium, sodium, boric and silica oxides)	
Ball clay	23.3
(A clay sourcing alumina and silica oxides)	
Silica	23.3
(Ground-up rock sourcing only silica oxide)	

If you were to type the recipe for glaze 9.1 into your glaze software, it would give you the following unity formula analysis:

Oxides in Glaze 9.1 after firing

CaO	0.44
Li_2O	0.15
MgO	0.37
K_2O	0.01
Na_2O	0.03
B_2O_3	0.06
Al_2O_3	0.32
SiO_2	2.35

SiO_2:Al_2O_3 ratio (2.35/0.32) = 7.34

If you were to mix up glaze recipe 9.1, you would weigh out the ingredients listed above in the recipe. Contained in these materials would be the atoms and molecules that would melt and re-form in the firing to create the oxides listed in the analysis. In the raw ingredients contained in the recipe, there would also be a lot of other atoms and molecules that you would not find in the list of fired oxides. Some would be driven off as a gas (steam, carbon dioxide, carbon monoxide or sulphur dioxide, to name a few), while others would rearrange to form new molecules during melting. If you want to do an experiment, try firing a weighed sample of any dry clay (or simply weigh any piece of dry pottery before firing) and then weigh it afterwards. Since clay contains chemically bound water as part of its molecular structure, as well as other molecules that are driven off by high temperatures, your piece will weigh less after firing than before.

What is a unity formula?

A unity formula is a nifty way of scaling the results of the formulation analysis to make them easier to compare with other tests. Since the numbers in the results are all relative amounts, they can be displayed differently as long as their ratios stay the same. By 'forcing' the flux oxide values to add up to unity, or 1.0, it's simpler to compare the relative amounts of silica and alumina to the fluxes than it might be otherwise. This is the standard way of displaying formulation results and makes it easier for one person to compare their results to someone else's. Glaze software does all this for you automatically.

If this is confusing, try to think about it in another way. What we are dealing with here are ratios: for every one of this sort of thing (flux oxides) we have so many of another sort of thing (silica, alumina, and other oxides that are NOT flux oxides). So, to use an example, if your kiln can hold 10 plates per firing, then that is a ratio of one kiln per ten plates, or one to ten. It would be equally true to say that two kilns could hold 20 plates, and this ratio could be described as two to 20. Also true would be the statement that half a kiln could hold 5 plates, the ratio here would be half to five. While all these ratios describe exactly the same relative numbers, I think you will agree that the first ratio, one to ten, is the most straightforward and the easiest to interpret quickly. That is all that is happening with the unity formula above: instead of the ratio being described in a complex way, by using a unity formula, the ratio is displayed in the simplest terms possible.

UNDERSTANDING THE RESULTS

The numbers in the oxide analysis for glaze recipe 9.1 opposite are relative average numbers of molecules. Just as the average number of children in families today is thought to be something like 2.2 even though you cannot actually have 0.2 of a child, so you also cannot have 0.44 of a molecule of calcium oxide, even though, relative to the other molecules, that is what you do have. To put the above list into words, you would say, 'For every 0.44 of a molecule of calcium oxide, you have 0.15 of a molecule of lithium oxide, and 0.37 of a molecule of magnesium oxide,' and so on. The oxide lists produced by

Glaze-formulation software will allow you to change an existing glaze in the following ways:

- Make a glaze runnier or stiffer
- Develop a matt glaze from a gloss glaze, and vice versa
- Change the flux oxide to change the colour response of a colourant
- Change the firing temperature (cone) of a glaze
- Replace an expensive or no-longer-available ingredient with another
- Bring a glaze within the limits to reduce leaching
- Increase or decrease the amount of crazing
- Enhance the glaze adhesion to your clay body to reduce the likelihood of crawling
- Replace ingredients that give off gases with those that do not, to reduce pinholing
- Use up old materials that have been lying about and that you are unsure how to use

Cathy Kiffney, *Prothonotary Warbler Tile*, 2009. 28 x 18 x 1.3cm (11 x 7 x ½in.). Developing your own glazes for your work can make the work really stand out, as in this tile. *Photo by the artist.*

glaze formulation software will never attempt actually to tell you how many individual atoms and molecules there will be in your glaze, as this would not only be difficult and unwieldy but also unnecessary. The important thing is the relative amounts, as this will most accurately describe the behaviour and characteristics of the fired glaze. This method of reporting the results is called a unity formula (see box opposite).

Additionally, the software will give you the ratio of silica to alumina molecules in the fired glaze. This is another value used to determine whether or not the glaze will 'work' (see the notes to Table 1 in the section on technical information at the end of the book for more information on this ratio).

Once the list of oxides is known, these values can be quickly compared to limit tables that have been developed to indicate whether or not the glaze will fire and melt at a given cone value. Your goal is to find out if your range of oxides will fall between the values in the limit tables.

If they do, then your theoretical glaze recipe is likely to work. If one or more of the oxide values fall outside the limits, it's fairly easy to change one or more of the raw ingredient amounts to make the oxide values increase or decrease as needed. It is as simple as that! Most of the software packages will provide limit tables for you, or you can develop your own based on glazes that you already have that you know to work at specific cones. You can then quickly compare new, untested glaze recipes to the oxide values you have, and see if the new glaze falls inside or outside those limits. Glazes that fall outside can be rejected without testing as being unlikely to work, or, better yet, adjusted to fall within the limits so as to improve their chances of success. (See Tables 1 and 2 in the technical section at the end of the book for limit tables specific to certain cone values.)

ALTERING GLAZE RECIPES

After you have used the software a bit and become familiar with how it functions, you can begin to use it to make changes to your existing glazes and even to develop some of your own. There are many reasons why you might want to make changes to an existing glaze. The list on the previous page gives you some ideas as to how you might use the software to make changes to an existing glaze.

So, if you have a glaze and it is not behaving properly, you can look at its chemistry and make strategic changes to adjust it. Most importantly, you can make these changes to the raw materials you are using in the glaze and instantly see the effect on the fired glaze chemistry, without having to fire any test tiles, although, of course, it is possible to make all these same changes using line-blending techniques as well – it will just take more time.

For another example of how to make changes to an existing glaze, let's take a look at glaze recipe 9.1 again. When comparing the chemistry of this glaze to the limits for cone 6 that appear in Table 1 in the section on technical information at the end of the book, we notice that a few of the oxides' values in the unity formula fall outside the suggested ranges for cone 6. Potassium and sodium added together only come to 0.04, which is below the 0.1 low value in the table. Magnesium oxide is slightly above the limits at 0.37. However, all the other oxides fall within the ranges provided. It is also important to check the ratio of alumina to silica. Even though the individual oxide values fall within the limits, it is still possible for there to be an imbalance between these two oxides, especially if one is towards the upper end of the published limits and the other is at the lower end. For all glazes at all cones, the ratio should be between 7 and 11. Certainly, a few glazes will work outside this range, but they will tend towards producing unusual results, such as crystalline glazes (low alumina). Our recipe's value of 7.34 falls within the range we are looking for.

If we wanted to 'correct' recipe 9.1 to bring it within the set limit-value range in order to improve its performance at cone 6, we could use the software to vary the amounts of the raw ingredients and instantaneously see what happens to the list of oxides. Even if we didn't know which raw material was a source of each oxide, the computer would not allow us to go too far off course. By increasing or decreasing the amount of any of the raw ingredients we could quickly see if we were changing the right material in the right way.

By working with the software for just a few minutes it is possible to come up with the following revised recipe that falls within the limits.

Glaze recipe 9.3 (recipe 9.1 corrected to fall within limits) cone 6

Dolomite	15.9
Spodumene	13.6
Frit 3134	15.5
Ball clay	33.9
Silica	21.1

Oxides in fired glaze 9.3

CaO	0.48
Li_2O	0.12
MgO	0.30
K_2O	0.01
Na_2O	0.09
B_2O_3	0.17
Al_2O_3	0.43
SiO_2	3.08

$SiO_2:Al_2O_3$ ratio $(3.08/0.43) = 7.2$

Glaze recipe 9.3 fired to cone 6. The reformulated glaze is clearer and fits the clay body better than the original (see image p.115). *Photo by Jennifer A. Siegel.*

David Stuempfle, *Jar*, 2009, 63.5 x 61cm (25 x 24in.). Wood-fired salt-glazed stoneware using local clay. Natural ash glaze from a five-day firing. *Photo by Tim Ayers.*

The relative increase in the amounts of sodium and potassium should give the glaze a more shiny finish with an enhanced colour response to any colourants added, while the slight decrease in magnesium oxide should result in only very slight changes to the finished glaze, which are likely to be unnoticeable. (For more information on the influences each flux oxide has on the finished glaze, see Chapter 5.)

Once you are familiar with how the software works, you can make changes to existing glazes very quickly. It is infinitely satisfying to be able to make good changes quickly to a glaze that has been problematic, especially when the changes work! Looking at glazes as overly complex and mystical formulations that are not to be messed with by mere mortals is a thing of the past. These days, even as beginners we have the ability to conquer our glaze-formulation fears and quickly get on with making good and useful glazes.

DESIGNING YOUR OWN GLAZES, FROM SCRATCH!

Once you have gained some familiarity with the software, you can start to truly realise its potential. Developing your own unique glazes for your work is as important as developing your own sculptures or pots. The entire process can now be personalised and developed to meet your goals!

When developing a glaze, it is good to answer a few preliminary questions that all relate to the overall question of 'What is it that I want?'. You'll find a number of dichotomies arise when making these choices, and these are listed below.

Lara O'Keefe, *Wood Fired Salt Glazed Jar*, 2008, 38 x 25cm (15 x 10in.). Choosing the right glaze can make all the difference. Red and white slips with rib designs and celadon glaze. Made from locally sourced clay. *Photo by Jason Dowdle.*

Matt	or	Glossy
Opaque	or	Transparent
Stable/ Leach-resistant	or	Stability is unimportant (See Chapter 5 for more information)
Crazed	or	Crack-free
Durable	or	Durability is unimportant
Bright colours	or	Muted tones

There are also two other questions to answer before you start:

- What cone do you plan to fire this glaze to?
- What colour do you want?

Limit tables will help you make a glaze that performs well at the cone you choose. Looking at Table 3 in the section on technical information at the end of the book, the Flux Oxide Colour Response Chart will help you determine which colouring oxides to use with your formulated glaze. The flux and colour table does not list the responses derived from using mason stains in your glaze, but the component colourants used in the stains are usually given in the suppliers' catalogues or can be found online. These can then be compared to the table.

For example, let's say we want to make a cone 6 glaze that is glossy, opaque, durable and blue-green. Looking at our cone 6 limit tables in Table 1 of the technical information section, we see that we will need the following oxides in our glaze: potassium and/or sodium, calcium, alumina and silica. For a nice gloss glaze we will want the silica:alumina ratio to be towards the upper end of about 11:1, since less alumina will make for a more complete melt. To make our glaze opaque, we will need to add an opacifier. Several exist that we can use, but the most common and inexpensive is one called Zircopax. It is usually added in amounts of up to 10%, with 7% giving a good opacity to most glazes. Our colour will come from copper carbonate, which gives green to blue results when in a glaze containing high proportions of sodium and potassium flux oxides, which ours does.

Nearly every glaze needs a clay, a frit or feldspar, silica and at least one additional source of flux in it (see Chapter 8). As we have seen, the clay is a source of some of the silica and alumina for the fired glaze, and the frit or feldspar is a source of more silica and alumina, plus any number of different flux oxides. For our clay, we will use a kaolin (china clay), as these clays tend to be low in iron, and, since we are trying to make a green glaze, iron will not be beneficial. Next we need to choose a frit or feldspar. For our purposes, we will choose Ferro Frit 3110, since it is high in sodium oxide and relatively low in calcium oxide, which will help to make the glaze a bit brighter (see Table 5 in the section on technical information at the end of the book; the glaze software you purchase will contain the chemical make-up of hundreds of raw materials, making this step a lot easier in practice). Using our glaze-formulation software, the following recipe can be developed:

Glaze recipe 9.4 blue-green-gloss-opaque glaze cone 6

Kaolin	22
Ferro Frit 3110	35
Whiting	13
Magnesium carbonate	4
Silica	26

Opacifiers and colourants

| Zircopax | 7% |
| Copper Carbonate | 2% |

Developing this glaze on the computer took about five minutes. Now it is just a matter of trying it out and refining it, which will usually involve some line-blending to tease out the exact look you are going for; the computer can only help with this so much. Above all, have fun being in charge of your own glaze making. Now the entirety of your work can become your own creation, with a lot less effort and a greatly increased chance of success.

Glaze recipe 9.4 fired to cone 6. *Photo by Jennifer A. Siegel.*

10

Firing Kilns

TYPES OF KILNS

Clay has been fired in many different kinds of kilns over the centuries. Early potters used whatever fuel was readily available to make heat, including animal dung, grass and wood. Their kilns were often no more than a pit dug in the ground, or simply a bonfire, which does away with the idea of 'kiln' almost completely. Over the centuries kiln designs changed as the understanding of heat concentration was better understood. Modern potters mostly rely on three types of fuel: wood, gas (propane and methane) and electricity. Wood and gas kilns are categorised by the direction of flame flow: updraught, downdraught or crossdraught. Some wood kilns also go by Japanese terms having to do with their shape: anagama meaning 'tube'-shaped kiln, naborigama for 'chambered' kiln, and so on. Many modern potters rely on several different types of kilns to achieve their goals. Some artists bisque-fire in an electric kiln and then glaze-fire in a gas, wood or raku kiln. This chapter will introduce some of the characteristics of each type of common kiln and provide information on which kiln might best serve a beginner clay artist.

CHOOSING A KILN

As has been touched upon earlier in this book, decisions made by clay artists around what kind of kiln to use depend on several factors. Probably the most important factor is the scale of the production. How many pieces will be made each year? High-quality electric kilns are available that hold just a few small pieces, so small productions usually best rely on electricity, as small wood-fired and gas kilns tend to be a lot more difficult to manage. Large productions can rely on large gas, wood or electric kilns depending on what kind of fuel is available to them.

The second and third factors that usually come into play when choosing a kiln involve the look of the finished pieces that the artist requires and the costs involved with the various types of kilns available. In electric kilns fuel is not burned, so creating 'atmospheric' effects on the ware during a firing is not possible. In gas- and wood-fired kilns, the burning fuel allows the operator to change the way the clay and glazes look through careful control of the burning process.

As far as cost is concerned, pre-manufactured kilns tend to be very expensive, regardless of the type of fuel. The cheapest are usually small electric kilns, followed by larger electric kilns, small gas-fired kilns and, finally, wood-fired kilns. The expense with wood-fired kilns comes from the fact that a large portion of the kiln must be set aside for the firebox and the chimney, thereby increasing the cost of the kiln without increasing its capacity to fire pieces. Similarly, gas-fired kilns normally have a 'flame channel' (where the burners are directed into the kiln and no pots can be stacked), plus a chimney. Building your own kiln can save a lot of money, but can also be a complex and exhausting task taking many weeks or even months to complete.

ELECTRIC KILNS

Electric kilns tend to be the easiest and safest kilns to install and operate. Normally they arrive on a truck and are set down in the location set aside for them. Simply plug in the kiln, press 'start' and you're off! The location you choose for the kiln is important, as there are several safety precautions to be aware of when locating a kiln.

Ventilation: the fumes given off by kilns are hazardous. The kiln should be situated in a space that is separate from normal work or living space. Electric kilns can be placed outdoors, in a rainproof enclosure. Situating a kiln outdoors eliminates hazards created by heat and noxious fumes. Indoors, the kiln must be situated away from heat-sensitive materials; it must be able to be locked away from people; and it must be in a space with active (mechanical) ventilation in combination with an adequate fresh-air inlet. Ventilation can be achieved simply with a fan in a window and an open door to allow fresh air to replace what is being removed. *Working in an enclosed space with an operating kiln without proper ventilation should never be allowed.* See Appendix 3 for more safety information.

Fire hazards: The exteriors of electric kilns get very hot. Nothing flammable should be stored within three feet of the kiln, and no flammable fluids should be stored in the same room as a kiln.

Electric-shock hazards: Electric kilns generally use a lot of electricity. Many have devices meant to ensure that the kiln is not 'on' when the lid or door is opened, but these can fail. Always be sure the kiln is off before opening. *Direct contact with an operating kiln element can be fatal.*

Burns: The exterior surface of electric kilns can become extremely hot. Make sure no one can come close to the kiln when it is operating. This may mean building a lockable enclosure for the kiln. *Accidentally opening a kiln when the interior is hot could be life-threatening.* Be sure to understand how to tell whether or not your kiln is cool before opening it.

An excellent book that describes well how to situate and operate electric kilns is *The Electric Kiln* by Harry Fraser (see the bibliography at the end of the book).

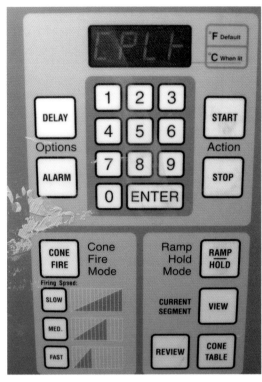

Keypad for electric kiln digital controller. The controller allows the user to use pre-set schedules or to develop and save their own.

A top-loading electric kiln with programmable digital controller.

Older kilns have very basic controls. *Photo by the author.*

Electric kiln controllers

Electric kilns utilise a variety of devices for controlling the rate of temperature change in the kiln and the manner in which it turns off. Modern electric kilns often combine these two capabilities in a computerised control unit.

These allow you to program the rate of temperature change in several segments, with the kiln automatically shutting off at the desired cone. While these controllers are expensive, they tend to pay for themselves quickly in saved electricity usage as the kiln never sits waiting for the user to show up and

change the dial! Older kilns often just have a 'low, medium, high' dial on the front and nothing more.

Kilns without computerised controllers can be adequately controlled by use of a pyrometer (a high-temperature thermometer) and pyrometric cones. Pyrometric cones are small cone- or

An analogue pyrometer.

Zone controls on an electric kiln.

bar-shaped pieces made to melt at specific cone values (see Chapter 4, p.p. 71–2). However, any kiln without a computerised controller or a kiln sitter will rely on someone being present to switch it off at the end when it reaches temperature.

Some electric kilns use a 'kiln sitter' for shutting off at a specific cone (see Chapter 4 for an image of a kiln sitter). To operate these, a pyrometric cone or bar is installed in a holding device inside the kiln. When the cone softens, it bends, triggering a lever which causes the kiln sitter to shut off the kiln. These incredibly handy devices are also very reliable, but have been all but replaced by computerised controllers in modern kilns.

If you do not have any other type of controller on your kiln, use your 'low, medium, high' knob (or knobs) and your pyrometer to turn up the kiln following one of the firing graphs provided in the table of cones and firing schedules at the end of the book. If you have more than one 'zone' in your kiln, or a specific section of heating elements controlled separately from other sections, sequentially turn up the kiln from bottom to top as the kiln heats, i.e. bottom to low, then middle to low, then top to low, followed by the bottom to medium, middle to medium, etc.

When approaching your final temperature, use a 'cone pack' situated in the kiln near a spy hole to tell you when the firing is complete. Remember to include this when you pack the kiln. Remember from Chapter 4 that temperature alone cannot tell you when a firing is complete. Use caution when peering into an operating kiln at high temperatures; it is easy to get a burn from the heat emanating from a spy hole, and it is highly recommended that you wear darkened safety glasses to protect your eyes from the intense light (these can be purchased from many ceramics suppliers).

Cone packs

A cone pack is simply a group of cones held in place by a wad of clay. To make one, at a minimum you will need at least three cones: your 'target' cone, or the cone that you wish to fire to, plus one cone above and one cone below your target. So, for example, for a stoneware firing to cone 10 you would need cones 9, 10 and 11, and for an earthenware firing you would need cones 05, 04 and 03. Many people choose to make cone packs with more than three cones in them so they can 'see' a broader range of heating effects during the firing. You get to choose how many to put in your packs.

Since you will be pushing these into wet clay, it is best to do this a few days ahead of firing to allow the clay to dry. As the clay used to make the cone pack will not be bisque-fired, for quick firings it is advisable to wedge some grog or sand into the clay to help it withstand the firing without exploding. Angle the cones so that as they melt they will fall one on top of the other, with the first cone to melt falling away from the others. The lowest cone will tell you when you are approaching the end of the firing, the target cone will melt when it's time to stop firing, and the highest cone will melt if you overfire. Don't forget to put in your cone packs before the firing begins! Check that the cones are visible through the spy hole with the door shut before you start. Use a flashlight or torch to see into the dark interior of the kiln if necessary.

During the firing, you will need to view the cones by pulling out a brick or a plug. Make sure that the cones are easy to see before starting the firing.

Depending on the size of your kiln, the residual heat inside it will continue to apply some 'heatwork' (see Chapter 4 for more information) to the pieces and the cones for a while after the kiln has been turned off. Stop the firing a bit before the target cone bends over completely in order to not overfire your pieces. With practice you will get to know how your kiln fires and how to set its controllers to get the results you are looking for.

A cone pack before firing. *Photo by Jennifer A. Siegel.*

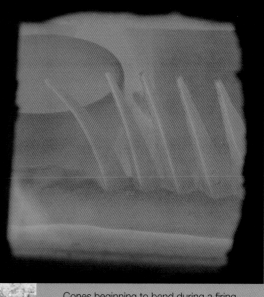

Cones beginning to bend during a firing. *Photo by Sheridan Ray courtesy of Joe Cole.*

Viewing the cones during a firing. *Photo by the author.*

Loading electric kilns

Most people who regularly fire electric kilns do two types of firings: bisque and glaze. Bisque firings are done with dry clay pieces with no glaze on them. The bisque firing is simply done to make glazing easier, and normally has little effect on the finished look of the ware. Since the pieces are unglazed, they can touch each other and the kiln in ways that must be avoided during a glaze firing. In fact, for efficiency's sake, many people 'tumble stack' their bisque ware. This means that the pieces are carefully piled up inside the kiln between the shelves, with attention being paid only to how fragile the pieces are and not their position. Doing this usually allows about twice the number of pieces to be packed in a bisque firing as in a glaze firing.

Bisque firings normally take about twice as long as glaze firings, even though they are (usually) fired to a lower cone value. This is because the chemical changes that are happening in the clay during a bisque firing need to be allowed to happen gradually, otherwise cracking and exploding can occur. Once these changes have happened, the clay can be fired much more quickly for a glaze firing, at least through the early stages. Take a look at the firing-schedule graphs in the table of cones and firing schedules at the end of the book for more information on how to plan your firings.

Loading unfired pieces in a tumble-stack fashion is fairly straightforward. Simply stack sturdy pieces on the bottom with gradually more delicate pieces on top of them. Finally, put in kiln posts (also known as kiln props) that are slightly taller than the stack of ware, and put a shelf on top of those, continuing to put more ware on top of that shelf until the kiln is full. Pieces should optimally not be any closer than an inch to the kiln's elements. Pieces should also be completely air-dry before being loaded into the kiln. Pieces that are slightly damp need to wait for another firing (because otherwise they will explode in the kiln).

above A loaded electric kiln before a bisque firing, illustrating how pieces can be in contact during this firing. *Photo by Jennifer A. Siegel.*

left A kiln partially packed with raw work showing how the kiln is packed using shelves and kiln posts (props) for each layer. *Photo by Jennifer A. Siegel.*

below A selection of kiln posts (props) used to support shelves during a firing. These are hollow square forms, but they can also be circular tubes.

Kiln wash or bat wash being applied to a kiln shelf. This can be purchased already mixed or you can make your own.

Loading glazed pots that have been through a bisque firing is just slightly more complicated than loading a bisque firing. First of all, the glaze on the pieces should not be allowed to touch anything. If glaze comes in contact with shelves or posts, it can be very difficult to remove after firing. To help preserve shelves, most people apply a few layers of kiln wash to the tops of the shelves prior to the first glaze firing. As bits of glaze become stuck to the shelf, they can be chipped off with a hammer and screwdriver or chisel and then wash can be reapplied to the damaged area. A recipe for kiln or batt wash is given in the back of the book.

The glazed pieces will expand slightly during the firing, so some space must be left around each piece so that glaze is not exchanged between pieces. The most efficient way to load a glaze firing is to put pieces of similar height together on one shelf, then put in kiln posts that hold the next shelf just about 1–2.5cm (½ – 1in.) above the tallest piece. Often this means a layer of mugs, followed by a layer of plates, followed by a top layer of vases. Each firing will be different depending on the various heights of the pieces going in.

Firing electric kilns

General information

Most electric-kiln operators choose to leave the top spy-hole of their kiln (if there is one) open during the entire bisque firing and nearly the entire glaze firings. This allows fumes to escape from the kiln without building up inside and condensing on the interior of the kiln's metal frame. Since the fumes that are driven off tend to etch metal and can cause chemical reactions with some metal coatings, it is best if they are allowed to leave the kiln through a spy hole where there is no metal present. If, however, you have installed a kiln ventilation system (a special set-up that mounts directly to the kiln itself and vents outside), then you should always leave all the spy holes tightly closed. During the final stages of glaze firings, when the kiln is working the hardest, many people plug the spy holes to increase efficiency. Even so, room ventilation fans should be run throughout the duration of firings to ensure safe indoor air quality.

Firing electric kilns: bisque firing

The first stage of firing has to do with drying out the pots and causing all the 'mechanical' water they embody to be emitted as vapour. To ensure that this happens completely, run the electric kiln with the spy holes open or (in the case of top-loading kilns) the lid propped up for several hours, but only if your kiln comes with a latching prop that keeps the situation safe for all users (see Chapter 4, p. 73 for an image of a kiln lid propped up). In bigger kilns, this early heating is often allowed to continue overnight, or for 8 to 10 hours. Be sure the temperature in the kiln does not go above 100°C (212°F) or the water in the pots can rapidly turn to steam and cause the pieces to explode! Maintain a temperature close to (but below) the boiling point of water; a

reasonable temperature to shoot for is about 85°C (185°F).

Next, begin to increase the temperature gradually (see the table of cones and firing schedules at the end of the book for firing-schedule graphs). There are several other changes that must occur during the first 600°C (1112°F) (see Chapter 4), so temperature increase must be gradual, about 83°C/hour (150°F/ hour if using °F). After quartz inversion, not much else happens to the clay and glaze until the latter begins to melt. Temperature increase can then be faster for a bisque from 600°C (1112°F) to completion. But where to stop? Remember that the main goal of bisque firing is to make glazing easier (and more successful). Have a look also at the normal firing schedule on p.155. However, bear in mind that some people don't bisque at all and get perfectly good results.

A pot that is well bisque-fired will have the following characteristics:

- Durable (will not disintegrate when wet)
- Porous and absorbent (not vitrified, so liquid glaze will cling to it when applied).
- Will off-gas very little during the glaze firing (organic materials and gas-releasing minerals will have been burned off or chemically changed sufficiently during the bisque firing to reduce the chances of pinholing during glaze firing).

For some low-temperature glaze firings that incorporate precise surface decorations (such as maiolica) it may well be advantageous to bisque-fire to the same cone or one cone higher than the subsequent glaze firing so as to minimise the gases that must pass through the melting glaze. Generally, though, having your bisque firing reach earthenware temperatures will usually suffice to meet the above criteria. This will be somewhere between cone 08 and cone 04. Try bisque-firing to several different cones before deciding on the one that works best for you.

Firing electric kilns: glaze firing

Glaze-firing schedules are somewhat easier to accomplish than bisque-firing schedules as there is no need for a long drying-out stage early on (except when single firing, where the bisque schedule and the glaze schedule get combined). The important part of a glaze firing is what happens around the peak temperature. Often there is some soaking – holding at a specific temperature for a certain length of time – to ensure the glaze completely melts and any imperfections have a chance to smooth out. Sometimes there is some annealing (slow cooling) after the peak temperature is reached to allow additional fusing with the clay body and possibly some crystal formation. For some examples see the firing schedules listed in the table of cones and firing schedules at the end of the book.

Electric kilns have a lot of advantages over other types of kilns. As mentioned earlier, these mainly have to do with their size and ease of operation. Another big advantage is how evenly they tend to heat their interiors. Unlike wood- and gas-fired kilns, where the heat is travelling through the kiln in one direction, electric heat is transferred to the pieces from all directions, as many electric kilns have elements all around the sides, the bottom and the top of the kiln. This even heating can greatly reduce damage to pieces and result in very uniform, predictable results. However, many artists want their kilns to have a bigger 'say' in the outcome of the firings. In other words, they want the heat and the fuel to affect the pots in unpredictable and non-uniform ways. Not having complete control is the goal!

Gas-fired and wood-fired kilns tend to fire in less predictable ways, and the results can be fantastic, though the losses can also be enormous.

GAS-FIRED KILNS

Gas-fired kilns can be large or small, and can be made of a variety of materials. Very small kilns, about 1 to 3 cubic feet (0.03 to 0.09 cubic metres), can be made of wire and ceramic fibre. Larger kilns tend to be made of various types of firebrick. Gas kilns require a source of pressurised fuel and one or more burners to mix the fuel with air and support a flame. There are a variety of types of burners, from simple pipe burners that rely on the pressure of the fuel to operate, to more complicated burners with blowers to control the airflow, to highly complex burners that are 'sealed' from the atmosphere and can precisely control the amount of air and fuel entering a kiln.

All gas-fired kilns require an exhaust port or chimney. In an updraught kiln, the kiln itself operates as a chimney, with the burners situated at the bottom and a port in the top functioning as the flue to allow exhaust fumes to escape. Downdraught and crossdraught kilns require a separate chimney to pull the exhaust gases from the kiln.

There are two main reasons why artists decide to use a gas-fired kiln instead of an electric kiln: the ability to (A) create a reducing atmosphere and (B) introduce flux oxides directly into the kiln during the firing. Reduction refers to 'reducing' the amount of oxygen available in the kiln to the colourants in the glazes and the clay bodies during a firing. Some of the colourants used in making ceramics respond differently depending on the amount of oxygen available to them as they melt! Copper is

probably the most extreme example. In the presence of oxygen, copper produces a greenish colour, while in the absence of oxygen, copper can produce reddish tones. Iron is also affected by reduction, changing from browns to greys and blacks as oxygen levels are reduced. Clay bodies are affected in the same way as the glazes, and those artists desiring a 'reduced' appearance to their work usually choose a clay body with adequate levels of iron oxide to produce the look they want.

Artists using gas-fired kilns can also introduce flux oxides to the atmosphere of their kiln during the firing. These firings are called salt or soda firings. More information about these types of firings can be found later in this chapter.

Loading gas kilns

Loading a gas kiln with pieces is done in the same way as for an electric kiln. Just like electric kilns, the shelving should have a layer of kiln wash applied to the top surface. Usually, if an electric kiln is available bisque firing is done in the electric kiln and glaze firing done in the gas kiln, since there is no benefit to bisquing in a gas kiln and operating gas kilns often requires more work on the part of the operator. Many people with gas kilns simply forgo bisque firing in favour of single firing. Applying glaze to a damp piece that is not rigid and strong like a bisque-fired piece takes some practice. Large pieces usually cannot be picked up at all, so glaze must be poured or sprayed. Moving these unfired pieces into the kiln can also be difficult. Some studios have kilns that can be built around large finished pieces of work, so that the need to move them when they are unfired is eliminated.

above left An 100 cubic ft (2.8 cubic m) gas-fired salt kiln. *Photo by Jennifer A. Siegel.*
left Gas burners raised on concrete blocks.
top right & above right Glazed pieces before and after firing in a gas kiln. *Photo by Jennifer A. Siegel.*

Firing gas kilns

If you are firing a home-made kiln, it is likely you will be dealing with high-pressure canisters of propane connected to burners. More permanent large kilns are usually connected to large propane tanks or hooked directly to the main gas line. Each burner will have a control to operate it. Some professionally manufactured gas kilns will come with computer controls to operate the burners and control the temperature gain in the kiln. Normally, determining the time to shut off a gas kiln will be done by viewing a cone pack through a spy hole, but some computer-operated kilns will do this as well, much like an electric kiln.

Oxygen sensors are sometimes installed in the exhaust flues or chimneys of gas kilns, allowing for precise control of the amount of reduction happening in the ware chamber. Traditionally, kiln operators have relied on other means to determine the degree to which reduction has occurred. Nearing peak temperatures, the amount of oxygen allowed to flow to the burners is gradually reduced, until a yellow flame instead of a blue flame can be seen in the flame channel. Adjustments are made to the damper in the chimney to change the rate at which exhaust fumes are able to exit. Black smoke usually begins to be emitted from the chimney as unburned fuel spills out of the kiln, and flames will start to show up, wiggling from every crack in the kiln as heated, unburned fuel escapes the oxygen-deprived chamber to burn in the oxygen available outside the kiln.

Allowing these signs of reduction to continue for a period of time near the maximum temperature of the kiln will cause the desired changes to occur in the ware, but each kiln is different, and the amount of reduction necessary to achieve the desired results will become known to the kiln operators only after a certain number of firings.

At the start of most gas firings, a single burner is ignited and allowed to slowly heat the kiln and the ware and dry everything out. Moisture being emitted from spy holes can usually be felt by hand. After several hours (sometimes many hours, depending on the size of the kiln) of warming and drying, the spy holes are sealed up and the remaining burners are ignited, one at a time, and slowly turned up. Now the watchful operator keeps an eye on the pyrometer and slowly turns up the burners, attempting to maintain a steady but gradual rise in temperature, usually 111–167°C/hour (200–300°F) if the pieces have been previously bisque fired. Near completion of the firing, safety glasses should be worn while cone packs are inspected. As the target cone begins to soften and bend, the burners are turned off; and the kiln is sealed up and allowed to cool.

Flames will appear out of cracks in a reducing kiln. *Photo by the author.*

WOOD-FIRED KILNS

Wood-fired kilns tend to be the most difficult and labour-intensive to fire of all kilns. A phenomenal amount of effort is involved in acquiring the wood, cutting it into the right size, drying it, stacking it, moving it, and then putting it into the kiln during the firing.

Choosing a wood kiln is also a huge undertaking as they cannot be bought ready-made and need to be built by someone. This requires a great deal of thought, study and design, as well as labour! There are many books on building wood kilns, and among the best are *The Kiln Book* by Frederick Olsen, *The Art of Firing* by Nils Lou, and Joe Finch's *Kiln Construction* (see the bibliography for more information). The detail on how to build a kiln unfortunately goes beyond the scope of this book.

Wood-fired kilns require constant attention throughout the firing, unlike electric and gas kilns, which once started can either be ignored until completion or just checked on periodically. Wood firing is a completely different kind of activity, and the amount of effort needed usually means that a community of artists works together to get all the jobs done. Wood-fired kilns also tend to be big. Kilns smaller than about 40 cubic feet (1.1 cubic metres) are unusual, whereas kilns larger than 100 cubic feet (2.8 cubic metres) are more common and often have more than one ware chamber. This means a large amount of effort is required simply to make enough pieces to fill the kiln, let alone fire it. Large wood firings thus commonly happen only a few times a year, with many people getting together for several days to participate.

Opposite right A large, multi-chambered wood kiln owned by Joe Cole. *Photo by Sheridan Ray, courtesy of Joe Cole.*
middle Large amounts of wood go into every wood firing. *Photo by the author.*
bottom Each piece in a salt, soda or wood firing must first have wadding attached to the bottom. *Photo by the author.*

Loading a wood-fired kiln

Like a soda or salt firing, wood firing requires that each piece loaded into the kiln is separated from the kiln shelves by a material called 'wadding'. Towards the end of a wood firing, the ash from the burning wood is sucked through the kiln by the draught. Part of the ash will vaporise and form a flux oxide-laden atmosphere which in turn causes silica in the pieces and in the kiln furniture to melt and form glass. Wood ash is made up of a variety of materials, but the main flux oxides found in most wood ash are calcium and potassium oxides. A certain amount of silica is also present in the ash, so at high temperatures bits of molten glass may be flying around inside the kiln, forming glaze on pots and potentially sticking everything together! The wadding prevents the pot from welding itself to the kiln shelf.

Since the pieces will be affected by the draught of wood ash and flux oxides coursing through the kiln during the firing, careful attention must be paid to how the kiln is loaded. The position of the shelves and the pieces will dictate the flow through the kiln, creating patterns on the surfaces. Packing the kiln tightly will reduce the amount of ash that builds up on the pieces, while a very loose stacking might not have enough structure to force the draught through the entire kiln. The loaders must 'think like fire' and position the pieces in the kiln so as to carefully dictate the flow of heat, gases and ash.

Firing a wood kiln

Once the kiln is loaded, the firing can begin. Wood kilns are often preheated overnight with a gas burner to help dry out the pots, glazes, wadding and cone packs, and to help start the draught up the chimney. Normally, after that it is just a matter of starting a small fire and slowly building up the temperature through the day. Having enough wood of the correct size for your kiln stacked close by in such a way as to make it easy to reach is vitally important. Wet or damp wood that is too big will cause the firing to come to a screeching halt. Lots of small pieces of wood will make stoking the fire a harder job, as the wood will be consumed very quickly at higher temperatures. A mixture of sizes is usually best, with the smallest dry wood stacked nearest the kiln so as to be used at the start, and larger pieces saved for the higher temperatures.

Once the kiln has passed the initial drying-out stage, it is important to get into a rhythm with the stoking. With each addition of wood, or each 'stoke', the kiln will go into reduction, meaning there will be more fuel in the system than oxygen needed for complete combustion. Smoke will be seen coming out of the chimney, and at high temperatures flames will be seen licking out of every crack and crevice of the kiln. After a short time, the smoke and flames will disappear and the kiln will be in a neutral state, meaning there is a balance between the amount of fuel and oxygen and the kiln will be heating efficiently. This is the time when the temperature in the kiln will rise. Following this, the kiln will go into an over-oxidised state, meaning that due to the draught more oxygen (air) will be flowing into the kiln and straight out of the chimney without combustion. This will only serve to cool the kiln.

With careful attention, the timing of the stoking will maximise the time period in the neutral stage, which in turn will maximise the temperature gain for the fuel used. Towards the end of the firing, again with careful attention, the kiln can be kept in a lightly reducing atmosphere to create

Stoking a wood-fired kiln. *Photo by the author.*

Flames circulating past the pots during a wood firing. *Photo by Sheridan Ray, courtesy of Joe Cole.*

effects on the pieces, if this is desired. Too much reduction and the pieces will be dull and potentially damaged; too little and the interesting effects of the flames and the atmosphere can be lost.

Sue Mulroy, Bowls, 2008, dia: 18cm (7 in.). On the exterior of these bowls can be seen the effects of wood ash from a wood firing. *Photo by the artist.*

An aqueous solution of salt and soda being sprayed into a gas kiln.

SALT AND SODA FIRINGS

As mentioned in Chapter 7, it is possible to introduce flux oxides during a firing with the intention of creating a glaze on pieces of work in the kiln. You must have a kiln that is specifically built for this use. The salt (table salt, or sodium chloride) and soda (baking soda, or sodium bicarbonate) that provide the flux oxides will eat into the kiln walls each time, coating the interior of the kiln with a sodium glaze. Normally, the salt and soda are introduced into the kiln near the peak temperatures, and for the biggest effect this is often in the vicinity of cone 10.

There are a variety of ways of introducing salt or soda into a kiln. In order to keep the majority of the material off the kiln floor, many kiln operators find it useful to spray the material into the kiln after first dissolving it in water.

Remember, however, if you do get the chance to do this sort of firing, to be very careful. *The fumes (chlorine) given off by vaporising salt can be deadly, and the heat from the kiln is intense and can easily severely burn you.* Wear good-quality cotton clothing, tie back hair, and wear eye protection and thick welding gloves. A gas mask rated for chlorine gas is recommended when introducing salt into a kiln, and this is available at many large hardware or DIY centres.

The amount of salt or soda required in any given firing will vary dramatically. A new, unseasoned kiln will require a lot more salt or soda than one that has been used many times before. Use 'draw rings' which are rings of clay positioned near the spy holes that can be removed during the firing with an iron rod, or keep a close eye on the pieces through the spy holes to determine how coated the ware has become. Use of draw rings gives the most accurate account of the extent to which the vapour in the kiln is creating a glaze on your clay body.

Be aware of the environmental hazards associated with salt and soda firings. The chlorine gas given off by salt

Draw rings removed from a kiln during the firing with an iron rod, used to see how the salt glazing was progressing. *Photo by Jennifer A. Siegel.*

firings is deadly. Soda firings are believed to be less toxic, but there is still debate about the health factors and the environmental damage associated with these two methods of firing.

Dan Rhode, *Pitcher*, 2005, ht: 25.5cm (10in.). Salt fired in reduction, cone 10. Interior glazed, exterior decorated with brush-applied black slip.
From the collection of E. Holloway.

RAKU FIRING

Potters and ceramic artists often work in solitary confinement in their studios with only the radio for company. Making clay pieces is not often thought of as a spectator sport, with crowds gathering for a viewing. But this is certainly not true when it comes to raku-fired ware! People love to watch raku pieces being fired. The process is quick, a bit dangerous, and involves high temperatures, molten glass, fire and smoke. Raku firing is a true crowd pleaser.

American raku firing developed from a method of rapid firing first practised in Japan. The American method is now what most people associate with the term 'raku', and is dramatic to witness. In simple terms, American raku firing is a fast firing during which the pieces are removed at peak temperatures from the kiln (when the glazes are molten) and are then subjected to 'post-firing reduction' (see the gas-fired kilns

section of this chapter for more information on reduction). Most people find that among the biggest drawbacks to making ceramic art are the long waiting periods involved. Raku shortens at least one of these periods dramatically. By rapidly heating the pieces, then removing them from the kiln for rapid cooling, the glaze-firing process can be shortened from tens of hours to about 30 minutes!

A variety of specialised equipment is needed to do raku firing. Normally, a basic requirement is a specially constructed raku kiln that allows the use of a powerful gas burner to heat a very small chamber, often just a single cubic foot or two (0.03 to 0.06 cubic metres) in volume.

The shell of the kiln is often made of metal and ceramic fibre, to make it very lightweight and easy to move. Easy-to-grab handles are built onto the sides, so the shell can be picked up and moved out of the way, leaving behind the exposed red-hot pieces, sitting on the

Helen Rondell, *Resist Slip Raku Form*, 2006, ht: 21cm (8¼in.). *Photo by Scott Wishart.*

A small raku kiln set up. *Photo by the author.*

A red-hot piece is removed from the kiln using long tongs. *Photo by the author.*

A raku piece is carefully lowered into a metal container containing wood shavings or paper for post-firing reduction. *Photo by the author.*

static base. Long-handled tongs are used to pick up the pieces, which are then carefully moved into a metal container with combustible material – often some newspaper or sawdust – at the bottom.

Once in the container, the combustibles ignite, and when the lid is sealed, a reducing atmosphere is created for a few moments around the piece, causing the colourants in the glaze and clay body to change.

A few minutes later, the colours have become frozen as the glaze hardens, and the still hot (but significantly cooled) piece can be removed from the container and, believe it or not, placed into another metal container filled with water for rapid cooling. A few minutes after that, the piece can be handled and admired!

right A fired raku piece being rapidly cooled with water. *Photo by the author.*

A raku piece seen inside a red hot raku kiln. *Photo by Libba Adams.*

Raku has its shortcomings, however. No piece of American raku-fired pottery should ever be used for food contact, for a number of reasons. The glazes used for raku tend to be incredibly colourant-saturated, making them very prone to leaching toxic colourants into, say, coffee. The low temperatures used also mean the clay bodies do not get vitrified, so they generally leak oil and water. And the post-firing reduction tends to leave burned carbon residue in cracks and crevices. If you are determined to do raku and use the ware for food, only use glazes with no colourants and with non-toxic fluxes (no lead, barium or lithium), and use natural combustibles (not newspapers due to the inks) in the reduction chamber. This will render the pieces a bit less interesting to look at, but the process will be the same, and will still be quick and fun to watch!

Raku firing is a highly dangerous activity and should only be done by individuals who have been trained how to do it safely. *Be very careful around the burner and the hose to the gas canister. Melting the hose or accidentally heating the canister could cause an explosion. Lighting the burner after there has been a gas leak can likewise be lethal. Severe burns can result from red-hot pieces toppling over as they emerge from the kiln. Fires that will engulf the whole area can be inadvertently ignited if combustibles are lit outside of containers.* Make sure the set-up is safe before starting, and have cool water to hand for cooling minor burns. Practise all the steps with the people participating before turning on the kiln for the first time, so that everyone knows where to be to stay safe and out of the way of the hot pots. Be sure people talk to each other while moving about with the hot pieces. Proper clothing and protective equipment (face masks, eye protection, gloves, boots, hair ties and cotton clothing in layers) are essential to having a good time.

Getting Started as an Artist

For many people, using this or other books to get a start as an artist making clay work will be accompanied by taking a series of classes at an art school. A few people will work from books alone, or learn the basics from a friend and then start to look around for some equipment of their own. Eventually, however, after the classes have ended or the helping friend has gotten too busy, the time comes to make pieces on your own. This can be a difficult transitional period. It often happens that budding artists start making art as a social outlet, and following their final class they simply wash off their wire tool and sponge and move on to other things. But for people that have a desire to continue with it, either as a hobby, semi-professionally, or as a full-time endeavour, keeping going on your own can be a daunting prospect.

WHERE TO BEGIN

Frequently, beginner artists are hindered by feelings of doubt and fear, which are, of course, perfectly normal feelings to have. Everyone attempting to do creative work on their own has these feelings from time to time, and they can be especially strong when first setting out.

As a first step, before committing to too much, make a plan. For those wanting to earn a living at art, this may eventually amount to a business plan, but it doesn't need to look like one, at least not yet. Write down a set of goals. Try to

above and opposite Artwork for sale at the North Carolina Craft Gallery, Carrboro, North Carolina. *Photo by Sara Gress.*

have some short-term (today or this week), medium-term (this month) and long-term (this or next year) goals. Post these somewhere that's easy to see every day, and amend and adjust them regularly. Be as specific as you can with these goals, and allow for flexibility and change within them. Be sure to check off the ones you accomplish, which will help give you the sense of accomplishment so desperately needed when working alone.

Table 5: Sample Goal List for the Avid Hobbyist		
Short-term	**Medium-term**	**Long-term**
Buy materials	Visit a new gallery	Take some more classes
Organize storage area	Find some reliable glaze recipes	Visit some local potters
Throw enough pieces to fill kiln	Put kiln wash on kiln shelves	Make some pieces to give away at holiday
Learn to bisque-fire by yourself	Organise glaze ingredients	Learn to decorate with underglaze

Table 6: Sample Goal List for the Developing Professional		
Short-term	Medium-term	Long-term
Buy clay	Complete pieces for gallery	Take raku workshop
Price pieces for sale	Replace kiln elements	Purchase new kiln
Call about show	Visit a new gallery	Make some low-fire ware
Pay bills	Develop new glaze recipes	Have pieces photographed
Mix glaze	Print business cards	Put together mailing list
Apply handles to mugs	Organise glaze ingredients	Build display stand

BE SOCIAL

Early on it is also a good idea to make some new acquaintances, this time relating to your interests as an artist, which may also be your new business. If you intend to sell your work, make an appointment with a gallery or shop owner who specialises in ceramic objects and ask them as many questions as possible about how to market and sell your work. Make appointments with a few professional artists (they don't have to be ceramic artists), too, and do the same. Keep these notes and work their suggestions into your list of goals. Be sure to spend time going to craft, art fairs and shows in your area to get to know how selling things is done. Hobbyists interested in expanding their knowledge would do well to simply visit galleries and artists, and do some sketching or note-taking about work that is of interest.

While visiting galleries, ask yourself what sort of work catches your eye, and how it is displayed or labelled. If you plan to go professional, there is no point

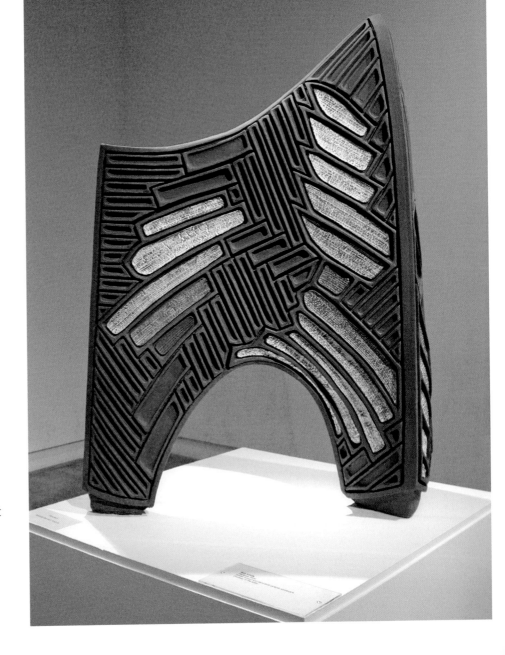

right Bob Kinzie, *Pegasus*, 2000, 101.5 x 66 x 31cm (40 x 26 x 12in.). Thrown hollow armature with textured thrown slabs cut and altered, and delineated by extrusions. *Photo by Sandy Kinzie.*

in reinventing the wheel when it comes to marketing and sales: look at what other people are doing and learn from their successes. This will free you up to get back to making things with clay as quickly as possible.

Everyone, regardless of their desire to sell their work, should consider ongoing art-related social activities, usually in the form of workshops or classes. Continuing to learn and develop by exposing yourself to new ways of working is nearly always beneficial, as long as you don't lose the vision you have for your own work.

RECORD YOUR SUCCESSES

Be sure to get in the habit of taking pictures of pieces that you have made that you like before you sell them or give them away. Post these pictures in your studio. They will help be reminders not only of where you have come from and how much you have developed; they will also help to jump-start your creative juices on days when no other ideas are coming. You might consider having professional images made of your best work; at some point you might need to produce marketing materials, and these are the images you will want to use. You could also make a note of the clay and glaze you used.

below left Salinda Dahl, *Primal Spring,* 2004–06, 51 x 23 x 20cm (20 x 9 x 8in.). Earthenware, fired to cone 04 with black manganese stain. Painted with acrylic paints after firing. *Photo by Seth Tice-Lewis.*

right Dawn Stetzel, *Tower,* 2007, ht: 1.8m (6ft). Birch leaves dipped in porcelain slip and then fired; the thin clay leaf impressions are stacked on a twig and peg structure. On the top (but not visible from this angle) is a porcelain cast egg. *Photo by the artist.*

FOR PROFESSIONALS: KEEP LEARNING (about your business!)

If you are serious about starting a full-time business, then it is a very good idea to take at least a few more classes, this time in marketing and small-business development.

You will need a good working business plan if you intend to go to a bank looking for a small business start-up loan, and these classes will help you make your plans realistic. You will also need a thorough budget plan and time horizon for making enough money to pay back the loans, for more information on starting an arts-based business, read *Crafting as a Business* (see bibliography).

Creating the plan will also help you think through all the resources around you. Where might you sell your work? How will you price things? How will you account for sales and deal with the legal aspects of running a business? It is a very good idea to get some of these issues sorted ahead of time, rather than waiting for problems to show up later.

far left May Criado, *Cabeza-piernas*, 2008, 7 x 7 x 27cm (2¾ x 2¾ x 10½ in.). Handbuilt porcelain, fired to 1250°C (2282°F). *Photo by Xose Abad.*
left Salinda Dahl sculpture on display in her studio garden. *Photo by the artist.*

KEEP PRACTISING

Most important while you are getting going on your new hobby or business is to remember to keep practising. Many potters have as an adage, 'touch clay every day'. As you progress into your practice, some of the shine will undoubtedly wear off. Some days will feel like a complete waste of time, or worse, you may feel you have actually gone backwards (such as when you open a kiln that has over-fired!). Look closely at the things that went wrong and try to determine when and how, so that you can avoid that mistake the next time.

right Throwing a pot on the wheel in a class. *Photo by Jennifer A. Siegel.*

BE REALISTIC

Remember as well to set yourself up for success. Try not to be too optimistic when getting started by, for instance, renting an expensive studio space with access to top-notch equipment. The stress imposed by these high costs early on might sour the experience so much that working with clay becomes a nightmare. Try to be realistic with your goals and timeline for getting going. Many people find putting a wheel in their kitchen and an electric kiln in the garage a good place to begin. Keep practising and make sure the practice is as fun and stress-free as possible. It is important to remember that the best pieces of art tend to come from people who make lots and lots of art. Almost no one makes just a few great pieces of art and then goes back to their job as a car salesman. Most artists practise everyday for years and years. Learning to enjoy the process, not getting hung up about the pieces that did not work out as planned, and practising every day will define who succeeds in the world of art and who does not. Success as an artist is not so much about talent as it is about practising and learning. A couple of good books to read on becoming creative and overcoming obstacles are *The Artist's Way* and *Art and Fear* (see the bibliography for details).

The initial phases of making art and learning your craft can be difficult. But improving at your craft and meeting others working in similar ways can be infinitely enjoyable. Most artists long remember their first successful pieces, the first time they made enough pieces to give some away as gifts, and their first sale. Who knows, choosing creativity as your life's work or hobby might just be the best decision you ever made!

top Mark Hewitt, *Iced Tea Ceremony Vessels*, 2008, ht: 20cm (8in.). Thrown with various decorative treatments including slips, melted blue glass, and salt glaze. Wood-fired. *Photo by the artist.*
above Bob Kinzie, *The Pond*, 2008, 30.5 x 40.5cm (12 x 16 in.). Made from thrown slabs which are cut up and assembled. Fired to cone 10 in reduction. *Photo by Sandy Kinzie.*

opposite
below Virginia Graham, *Chintz Rim Jugs*, 2008, ht: 19cm (7½in.) and 13cm (5in.). Stoneware clay, porcelain, and applied metal handles. Fired four times: biscuit, glaze, decal and lustre firings, with the biscuit firing the highest temperature. *Photo by Toril Brancher.*

APPENDICES

Appendix 1: Technical Information

Table 1: Unity formula limit values			
Oxide	Cone 04	Cone 6	Cone 10
CaO	0.1–0.6	0.2–0.7	0.3–0.8
KNaO*	0.3–0.6	0.1–0.4	0.0–0.3
MgO	0.0–0.1	0.0–0.3	0.0–0.4
ZnO	0.0–0.1	0.0–0.3	0.0–0.4
BaO	0.0–0.1	0.0–0.3	0.0–0.5
SrO	0.0–0.2	0.0–0.3	0.0–0.4
Li_2O	0.0–0.4	0.0–0.2	0.0–0.1
B_2O_3	0.0–0.8	0.0–0.5	0.0–0.3
Al_2O_3	0.1–0.3	0.2–0.5	0.3–0.6
SiO_2	1.5–2.5	2.5–4.0	3.5–6.0

Table 2: Colourant limits for reduced leaching	
Colourant	Maximum % of base glaze to use for stability (low leaching) at cone 6
Copper carbonate	4.0
Copper oxide	2.0–2.5
Chromium oxide	3.0
Cobalt carbonate	3.0
Cobalt oxide	2.0
Iron oxide	10.0–15.0
Manganese dioxide	4.0
Nickel oxide	3.0

(Above table adapted from Hesselberth and Roy, *Mastering Cone 6 Glazes*, 2002.)

*Sodium oxide (Na_2O) and potassium oxide (K_2O) values have been combined, with their individual values summed together. It is common practice for glaze-formulation software to give these as a combined number, as the chemistry of these two oxides is virtually identical when it comes to developing ceramic glazes.

Notes:
For all glazes at all cones, SiO_2:Al_2O_3 ratios are normally between 7:1 and 11:1. Both alumina and silica amounts relative to fluxes decrease for low-fire glazes and increase for high-fire glazes. Glazes with low ratio values (7:1–8:1) will be high in alumina and low in silica, and will tend to be stiffer, less glossy glazes (potentially 'alumina matt'). Glazes with high ratio values (10:1–11:1) will be high in silica and low in alumina, and will often be a bit runnier and glossier, but may end up matt if slow cooling creates micro-crystals (crystalline matt).

Hesselberth and Roy's recommended unity formula limit values at cone 6:
(From Hesselberth and Roy, *Mastering Cone 6 Glazes*, 2002):

CaO	0.2–0.6	B_2O_3	0.0–0.3
KNaO	0.1–0.3	Al_2O_3	0.25–0.5
MgO	0.0–0.3	SiO_2	2.5–4.0
ZnO	0.0–0.2		
SrO	0.0–0.2		

Notes:
Higher-temperature glazes are able to safely contain somewhat higher percentages of colourants than lower-temperature glazes as they necessarily contain a lower ratio of fluxes to alumina and silica. Alumina and silica tend to bind colourants more permanently than the fluxes, making for a more stable glaze (with less risk to food).

Stable matt glazes can be made, but it is important to ensure that mattness is achieved not through underfiring a glaze but through the creation of micro-crystals. Some fluxes (BaO, SrO, CaO, MgO, ZnO) develop micro-crystals more readily than others. Generally, to make a gloss glaze matt AND keep it stable, when developing your glaze reduce the amount of alumina to the bottom of the allowable range, and slow down the cooling of the kiln after reaching peak temperature (annealing). See the next section on cones and firing schedule suggestions.

Table 3: Flux oxide colour response

		COLOURANTS							
SOURCE	CuO Cu₂O Copper or Copper Carbonate	Fe₂O₃ FeO Red Iron oxide Black Iron Oxide	CoO Cobalt Oxide	MnO Manganese Dioxide	NiO Nickel Oxide	Cr₂O₃ Chrome Oxide	Rutile Rutile	V₂O₅ Vanadium Pentoxide
Toxicity as raw powder	Medium-high	Low	Medium-high	High	High	High	Low	High
BaO	Blue	Brown	Blue-green	Brown	Brown	Green	Multiple browns	Brown
CaO	Green *Red*	Yellow/ Black *Celadon*	Blue	Brown	Tan	Grass-green	Multiple browns	Brown
Li₂O	Blue	Brown	Blue	Purple-blues	Yellow	Green	Multiple browns	Brown
MgO	Green *Red*	Brown	Lilac	Brown	Green	Green	Multiple browns	Brown
K₂O	Bright green/ Blue *Red*	Black/ Brown/ Red *Blue* *Celadon*	Blue	Pink/ Purple *Brown*	Pink	Green	Brown/ Gold *Blue*	Yellow
Na₂O	Bright green/ Blue *Red*	Black/ Brown/ Red *Green*	Blue	Blue/ Purple *Brown*	Pink	Green	Brown/ Gold *Blue*	Yellow
ZnO	Green *Red*	Brown	Blue	Brown	Blue	Brown/ Orange	Orange/ Tan	Brown
SrO	Green *Red*	Brown	Blue	Brown	Brown	Green	Multiple browns	Brown
B₂O₃	Green *Purple*	Brown/ Green	Blue	Purple-blues	Brown	Green	Multiple browns	Brown

(Left margin label: FLUX OXIDES)

Notes on Table 3:

1. This chart depicts the colours that are likely to develop in glazes containing the flux oxides listed at the left—in the column starting with BaO. As an example from the chart, if you were to add red iron oxide to a glaze containing primarily ZnO (zinc oxide) as its flux component, the colour response after firing will be brown.

2. Italics indicates colour response in reduction. Where no italics are listed, reduction results tend to be the same as in oxidation.

3. Rutile is a combination of colourants, mostly iron and titanium. It tends to function as a variegator in most glazes.

Table 3a: Typical amounts of colourants to be added to a glaze

Oxide	Quantity
Cobalt carbonate	0.5–3%
Cobalt oxide	0.1–0.5%
Chrome oxide	0.5–2%
Copper carbonate	2–4%
Iron oxide	2–6%
Manganese dioxide	2–4%
Nickel oxide	1–5%
Rutile	1–5%
Tin Oxide	2–5%
Zirconium oxide	5–10%

4. Although not listed in the table, titanium dioxide (TiO_2), zirconium oxide (ZrO_2), and tin oxide (SnO_2) are all considered opacifiers; they make glazes turn white (opaque) regardless of the flux oxide present. Zirconium oxide is usually sold by the trade name Zircopax, and is used in percentages below 10% of the other dry ingredients. Tin oxide is much more expensive than zirconium, but is used in lower percentages, usually below 5% of the dry weight of the other ingredients. Tin is the classic opacifier used in maiolica glazes. Titanium dioxide is seldom added alone as an opacifier, but shows up in combination with other colourants, usually rutile, creating a mottled effect.

5. Crocus martis ($FeSO_4$) is a colourant used as a source of red iron oxide, but also contains other impurities and the iron particles in it can be of varying sizes which can result in speckling. Low toxicity.

6. Yellow ochre ($Fe(OH)_3$) is an impure form of red iron oxide and can be used as a substitute for it. Low toxicity.

7. Iron chromate ($FeO(Cr_2O_3)$) is a combination of iron and chromium (chrome) and can be used to produce gray, brown, and black colours. Highly toxic.

Table 4: Glaze ingredient information

Ingredient	Expansion coefficient (higher values will lead to crazing)	Particle size (an indication of whether or not the material will sink or suspend in the glaze bucket) VS=very small S=small M=medium L=large VL=very large	Will material evolve gas during firing? (can lead to pinholing)	Key oxides in each material	Sourced from	Function in glaze/Type of material
#6 Tile clay	5.1	S suspend	yes	SiO_2 & Al_2O_3	clay mines	clay
Alberta slip	6.8	S suspend	yes	SiO_2 & Al_2O_3	clay mines	clay
Alumina hydrate	6.4	L sink	yes	Al_2O_3	mined	stabiliser
Barium carbonate*	12.9	M sink	yes	BaO	mined	flux
Bentonite	5.4	VS suspend	yes	SiO_2 & Al_2O_3	volcanic ash	clay
Bone ash**	8.4	soluble suspend	yes	CaO & P_2O5	animal bones	flux
Borax	14.1	soluble suspend	yes	B_2O_3 & Na_2O	manufactured	flux
Cornwall stone (soda feldspar)	6.6	M sink	no	SiO_2 & Al_2O_3 & Na_2O	ground granite	glass former
Custer (potash feldspar)	8.1	M sink	no	SiO_2 & Al_2O_3 & K_2O	ground granite	glass former
Dolomite	9.7	L sink	no	CaO & MgO	ground limestone	flux
EPK (Edgar Plastic Kaolin)	5.0	M sink	yes	SiO_2 & Al_2O_3	clay mines	clay
Kona F4 (soda feldspar)	8.1	M sink	no	SiO_2 & Al_2O_3 & Na_2O	ground granite	glass former
Frits: 3195, 3110, 3124, 3134	9.2, 10.3, 7.7, 9.3	VL sink	no	several	ground glass	several
Gerstley borate	9.2	S suspend	yes	B_2O_3	mined	flux
Grolleg (English china clay)	5.4	S suspend	yes	SiO_2 & Al_2O_3	clay mines	clay
Lithium carbonate*	6.8	M sink	yes	LiO	mined	flux
Magnesium carbonate	2.6	M sink	yes	MgO	mined	flux
Nepheline syenite (soda feldspar)	9.3	M sink	no	SiO_2 & Al_2O_3 & Na_2O	ground granite	glass former
OM4 ball clay (Old Mine #4)	5.1	S suspend	yes	SiO_2 & Al_2O_3	clay mines	clay
Petalite (lithium feldspar)	4.3	M sink	no	SiO_2 & Al_2O_3 & LiO	ground granite	glass former
Redart clay	6.2	S suspend	yes	SiO_2 & Al_2O_3	clay mines	clay
Silica	3.5	L sink	no	SiO_2	quartz mines	glass former
Soda ash**	38.7	soluble suspend	yes	Na_2O	mined	flux
Spodumene (lithium feldspar)	4.6	M sink	no	SiO_2 & Al_2O_3 & LiO	mined	glass former
Strontium carbonate	13.0	M sink	yes	$SrCO_3$	manufactured	flux
Talc	3.2	M sink	yes	MgO	ground rocks	flux
Volcanic ash**	4.9	soluble suspend	yes	several	volcanic	glass former
Whiting	14.8	L sink	yes	CaO	mined	flux
Wood ash**	15.7	soluble suspend	yes	several	fireplaces	flux
Zinc oxide	9.4	M sink	yes	ZnO	smelting metal	flux

* More toxic ingredient   ** Caustic ingredient; damaging to skin

Table 5: Frit and feldspar chemistry/unity formulas

Ferro Frit 3110

CaO	0.29
K₂O	0.06
Na₂O	0.64
B₂O₃	0.09
Al₂O₃	0.09
SiO₂	3.00

A frit low in alumina, containing boric oxide
Also sold as Potclays Frit 2266

Ferro Frit 3124

CaO	0.69
K₂O	0.02
Na₂O	0.28
B₂O₃	0.54
Al₂O₃	0.26
SiO₂	2.55

A frit low in sodium and potassium,
containing boric oxide
Also sold as Potclays Frit 2272

Ferro Frit 3134

CaO	0.68
Na₂O	0.31
B₂O₃	0.63
SiO₂	1.47

A frit with no alumina containing boric oxide
Also sold as Potclays Frit 2273

Ferro Frit 3195

CaO	0.68
Na₂O	0.31
B₂O₃	1.09
Al₂O₃	0.40
SiO₂	2.75

A frit high in boric oxide and calcium
Also sold as Potclays Frit 2269

Potclays Frit 2263

CaO	0.63
K₂O	0.03
Na₂O	0.33
B₂O₃	0.63
Al₂O₃	0.17
SiO₂	1.88

A frit high in calcium and boric oxide

F-4 Feldspar

CaO	0.15
K₂O	0.27
Na₂O	0.56
Al₂O₃	1.04
SiO₂	6.15

A 'soda' feldspar; will melt to a glass at
cone 6

Nepheline Syenite

K₂O	0.25
Na₂O	0.74
Al₂O₃	1.10
SiO₂	4.65

A feldspar with a high potassium and
sodium oxide content

Cornwall (Cornish) Stone

CaO	0.30
Na₂O	0.34
K₂O	0.35
Al₂O₃	1.07
SiO₂	8.10

A feldspar with relatively high amounts
of calcium

Custer Feldspar

CaO	0.03
Na₂O	0.30
K₂O	0.64
Al₂O₃	1.04
SiO₂	7.13

A 'potash' feldspar

FFF Feldspar

CaO	0.03
Na₂O	0.45
K₂O	0.50
Al₂O₃	1.05
SiO₂	6.26

A mix of several 'soda' and 'potash'
feldspars

Forshammer Feldspar

CaO	0.07
Na₂O	0.62
K₂O	0.30
Al₂O₃	1.01
SiO₂	6.32

A 'soda' feldspar very similar to Custer
and F-4

Appendix 2: Cone Table and Firing Schedules

Orton cone table

The rate at which your kiln is increasing in temperature for the last 100°C (180°F) of a firing will determine the temperature at which your final cone will be achieved. Faster rates of temperature increase require higher final temperatures to achieve the same cone value. For a description of cones, temperatures and heat work, see Chapter 4.

Cone number reached at listed temperature	Values in °F			Values in °C		
	108° increase in final hour	270° increase in final hour	540° increase in final hour	60° increase in final hour	150° increase in final hour	300° increase in final hour
08	1728	1749	1801	942	954	983
07	1783	1805	1846	973	985	1008
06	1823	1852	1873	995	1011	1023
05	1886	1915	1944	1030	1046	1062
04	1940	1958	2008	1060	1070	1098
03	1987	2014	2068	1086	1101	1131
02	2014	2048	2098	1101	1120	1148
01	2043	2079	2152	1117	1137	1178
1	2077	2109	2163	1136	1154	1184
2	2088	2124	2174	1142	1162	1190
3	2106	2134	2185	1152	1168	1196
4	2120	2158	2208	1160	1181	1209
5	2163	2201	2230	1184	1205	1221
6	2228	2266	2291	1220	1241	1255
7	2259	2291	2307	1237	1255	1264
8	2277	2316	2372	1247	1269	1300
9	2295	2332	2403	1257	1278	1317
10	2340	2377	2426	1282	1303	1330

For example, if your kiln was increasing in temperature at 270°F per hour during the last 180°F of the firing, and fired to a maximum temperature of 2014°F, then the cone value achieved would be 03.

For reproducible results, care should be taken to ensure that cones are set in a plaque with the bending face at the correct angle of 82° from the horizontal, with the cone tips at the correct height above the top of the plaque, (for large cones this means 5cm/2in.).

Rates of increase per hour were maintained over the last several hundred degrees of temperature rise. It is not necessary to maintain this rate of increase over the entire firing cycle.

Information from the Orton Cone Company: www.ortonceramic.com

Firing schedules

The following graphs give an indication of how to fire a kiln to achieve certain results. Each kiln will be different, and the kinds of pieces in the kiln will influence the firing schedule. Thick pieces will require a somewhat more gradual schedule than thin pieces. Bisque firings (or single firings) take longer as more changes have to happen to the pieces during the firing. Glaze firings filled with bisque ware can be accomplished quickly, for example, raku firings are done in a matter of 15–20 minutes!

The glaze schedules depicted in the graphs are to cone 6, except the reduced pinhole schedules, where cones 04 and 10 have been added for comparison. From these graphs you can deduce that the schedule for any cone value is broadly the same.

Final temperatures for each graph are included as rough guidelines to follow.

Cone packs should be included to ensure that the proper cone has been reached.

The vertical axis for each graph is given in °F. To convert the major labels to °C use the following conversion chart:

°F	°C
500	260
1000	538
1500	816
2000	1093
2500	1370

Normal Firing Schedules

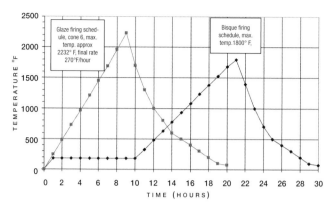

Reduced Crawling Firing Schedules

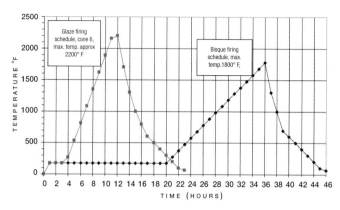

Reduced Pinhole Firing Schedules

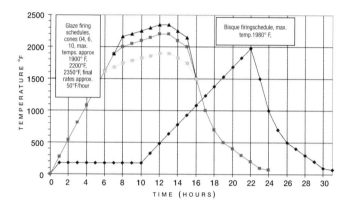

Enhanced Matte-Glaze Firing Schedule

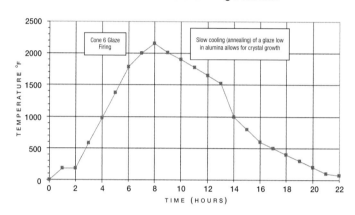

Appendix 3: Studio Safety and Environmental Health

Safety issues have been discussed throughout this book as they pertain to each aspect of making things with clay. Here are some other ideas to keep in mind to keep yourself and others safe.

Keeping the studio air clean

Throughout this book ideas have been mentioned about how to reduce or limit the amount of harmful dust and fumes present in a studio. Pay attention to this as part of your regular day-to-day studio upkeep. Clay dust can cause silicosis. Glaze dust can cause metal toxicity. Kiln fumes can cause emphysema, bronchitis and allergic reactions, or worse. Two good books to read concerning safety issues in the ceramics studio are *Safety in the Ceramics Studio* by Jeff Zamek, and *Artist Beware* by Michael McCann (see the bibliography).

Remember to wet-mop, never dry-sweep, the studio. If possible, hose down and use a squeegee on the floors, and wet tables down and soak up the water with a large sponge. Whenever possible, clean up wet clay spills before they dry.

Wash tools and equipment in a dedicated clay sink as much as possible and try to clean up your equipment before the clay dries.

Install exhaust fans near kilns or put kilns outside.

If you can afford it, install a filtration system to eliminate clay dust from the air (this should be common practice at schools and universities, but is often overlooked). Remember to change the filters regularly.

Keep windows and doors open whenever the weather will permit.

When raw materials arrive, transfer them from the paper bags they are shipped in into buckets or other rigid dispensing containers; this will minimise the amount of dust made airborne during use.

Don't forget to wear safety gear including rubber gloves, eye protection and dust masks when dealing with hazardous materials, including dry dusty materials. Wear an approved dust mask whenever you are producing dust. If possible, do these activities outside. A dust mask labelled N95 or N100 will work well to remove airborne clay-dust particles. Purchase one with an exhalation port in the middle for additional comfort and longevity. Do not use cheap, disposable, paper dust masks as they will not seal sufficiently nor remove small, hazardous particles.

Kiln-firing safety

During a firing, many different types of fumes are emitted, which can include: carbon dioxide, chlorine, fluorine, ozone, carbon monoxide, sulphur dioxide and metal vapours. Metal vapours can be produced by clays or glazes containing copper, zinc, brass, bronze, nickel, iron, manganese, lead, cadmium, antimony, barium, cobalt, lithium, vanadium and magnesium. These fumes are emitted at different stages of the firing, and in differing amounts depending on what kind of kiln it is (electric or fuel-burning) and what sorts of materials are in the kiln. **Therefore, it is imperative that all indoor kilns be vented directly to the outdoors.**

Kilns also pose fire and burn threats. Be sure to post signs indicating the risk and make sure that young children or other at-risk populations cannot gain access to raw materials, kilns or fumes emitted during a firing. Ensure that all flammables are kept away from kiln rooms.

'Green' studio habits

One aspect that is nearly always left out of books about clay is what do to with your waste. A lot of waste products are created during the making of clay pieces, and these arise at every stage of the process, from washing your tools and hands in the sink, to cleaning up in the glaze room, to discarding broken fired pottery. Here are some ideas to follow for those interested in reducing their impact on the local environment.

Users of any studio should attempt to designate a sink solely for cleaning up clay and another sink solely for cleaning up glazes. At the clay sink, since clay is harmless to the environment, it is OK for the clay simply to go down the drain. A fine screen over the drain will reduce the likelihood of clogs. Some studios have a settling container for clay below the sink, but these containers will give off a very unpleasant smell in a short space of time as bits of organic matter start to rot. This manner of collection, unless mandated by your local authority, seems pointless.

Under the glaze sink, however, it is certainly important to have a settling tank. Raw glaze materials should never go down into the regular drainpipes, as they are very difficult to remove later and usually end up directly out in nature. The colourants and flux oxides used for making glazes can be highly toxic, and should be disposed of carefully. When the settling tank gets full, remove any excess water. At this point you have two options:

(1) Use the collected glaze 'soup' to make a 'mystery' glaze and apply it to your pieces. A fired glaze that is even slightly glassy is a much safer alternative for disposal than the raw unfired ingredients.

(2) Dry it out (you can use cat litter, which is just lumps of clay, to speed up drying), and then put it in your rubbish bin. This keeps it from going directly into the water supply, and away from sensitive water ecosystems.

These are your same options when dealing with waste glazes from glaze tests, or old glazes that are just not going to be used anymore. Sometimes, local schools and ceramic clubs will accept old glazes as a way of saving money, but be sure to let them know what is in the glazes so they can make an informed decision about how to safely use them.

Appendix 4: US and UK Ceramic Terminology Equivalents

US TERMS	UK TERMS
Silica (not silica sand)	Flint; quartz
Grolleg; kaolin	China clay
Banding wheel	Whirler/banding wheel
Zircopax	Zirconium silicate
Kilnwash	Batwash
Loop tool	Strip tool
Glazing tongs	Glazing claws
Kiln posts	Kiln props

Appendix 5: Recipes

Most ceramic glaze recipes are written so as to add up to 100 of whatever unit (grams, ounces, pounds, etc.) is being used. Colourants are normally added on in addition to this total as a percentage, and are listed as such in the recipes below. See Table 3a in Appendix 1 for information on the recommended amount of colourants to add to the glazes below.

General-purpose underglaze
(cone 04–6)

OM4 Ball clay	50
Silica	30
Frit 3124	20

This recipe can be used to make a plain white underglaze into which colourants can be added. It fires nicely from earthenware to stoneware temperatures, but the amount of frit can be changed to help it adhere to the piece better at a given temperature (more frit for lower temperatures, less frit for higher temperatures).

Raku glazes

White crackle

Gerstley borate	78
Nepheline syenite	22

A classic white raku glaze that shows off the post-firing-reduction nicely as dark lines in the cracks that form.

Copper crackle

Gerstley borate	65
Nepheline syenite	21
Kaolin	4
Silica	10

Add 5–10% copper carbonate
A strongly coloured glaze that flashes to gold, yellow and red where the copper is reduced.

Low-fire glazes

Maiolica (cone 04)

Frit 3195	65
F-4 feldspar	18
Nepheline syenite	7
Kaolin	10

Add 8% tin oxide
A classic-looking maiolica glaze: rich milky white that takes on maiolica stains nicely. Maiolica stains can be made simply by combining most mason stains with equal parts ferro frit 3195 and mix in with water. See also p.104.

Clear glaze (cone 04)

Gerstley borate	48
Kaolin	8
Silica	19
Nepheline syenite	25

A variety of colourants can be added to this glaze with good results.
Try 1% cobalt carbonate for a deep blue, 1-2% copper carbonate for green, or any mason stain, usually in the range of 1-5%.

Mid-range stoneware glazes

Hare's fur (cone 6)

Nepheline syenite	47
Gerstley borate	28
Silica	20
Kaolin	5

A variety of colourants can be added to this glaze with good results. The glaze has a silky fur-like quality to it. Try 0.25% cobalt oxide, 3% iron oxide or 1% copper carbonate.

Bone (cone 6)

Frit 3195	30
Wollastonite	19
Nepheline syenite	16
Kaolin	16
Silica	19

Add 6% rutile
A soft and subtle off-white glaze. Other colourants can be used for different effects.

High-fire stoneware glazes

Transparent (cone 10)

Kaolin	20
Custer feldspar	25
Wollastonite	20
Zinc oxide	5
Silica	30

A variety of colourants can be added to this glaze with good results.

Celadon (cone 10)

Custer feldspar	25
Whiting	12
Kaolin	23
Silica	33
Dolomite	7

Add 3% iron oxide
Fired in reduction, this iron-bearing glaze will turn a celadon green.

Miscellaneous mixtures

Kiln wash (bat wash) for kiln shelves and posts

Alumina hydrate	60
Kaolin	40

Mix with water to a thin slurry. Can be applied with a brush or roller. Apply several thin layers rather than one thick one, to help avoid flaking. If flaking continues to be a problem try calcining (pre-firing) the kaolin first.

Wadding for soda, salt and wood firings

People use a variety of mixtures for their wadding, depending on what they prefer. Generally speaking, the mix is just alumina hydrate and kaolin, just like for kiln wash. More clay will help it stick better. Some people add other materials that burn out during the firing that help make remove of the wads easier, such as flour or sawdust. Sand can be added to help support heavier objects, as well as grog. For starters, try the kiln wash recipe above, just add less water to make a sticky paste.

Bibliography

Books

Bayles, D., and T. Orland (2001). *Art and Fear*. Image Continuum Press, California, USA.

Bliss, G. (2001) *Practical Solutions for Potters,* Sterling Publishing, New York, USA.

Botterill, C. (2001) *Clay For People With Special Needs,* A&C Black, London, UK.

Cameron, J. (2006). *The Artist's Way*, Jeremy P. Tarcher Publishing, New York, USA.

Cooper, E. (2000). *10,000 Years of Pottery*, University of Pennsylvania Press, Philadelphia, USA.

Finch, J. (2006). *Kiln Construction*, A&C Black, London, UK.

Fraser, H. (2006). *The Electric Kiln: A User's Manual.* A & C Black, London, UK.

Hesselberth, J., and R. Roy (2002). *Mastering Cone 6 Glazes.* Glazemaster Press, Pennsylvania, USA.

Hopper, R. (2004). *Making Marks* (K.P. Books, Iola, WI, USA.

Ilian, C. (1999). *A Potter's Workbook*, University of Iowa Press, USA.

Lou, N. (1998). *The Art of Firing*, A&C Black, London, UK.

McCann, M. (2005). *Artist Beware*, The Lyons Press, Connecticut, USA.

Mithen, S. (2004). After *The Ice: A Global Human History 20,000–5000 BC*, Phoenix Publishing, USA.

Olsen, F. (2001). *The Kiln Book* (3rd edition), A&C Black, London, UK.

Rhodes, D. (1973). *Clay and Glazes for the Potter,* Chilton Book Co., Pennsylvania, USA.

Rosen, W. (1998). *Crafting As A Business,* Sterling, UK.

Zamek, J. (2002). *Safety in the Ceramics Studio.* Krause Publications, Wisconsin, USA.

Suppliers

UK

Bath Potters Supplies Ltd.
Unit 18, Fourth Avenue
Westfield Industrial Estate
Radstock
BA3 4XE
Tel: 01761 411077
www.bathpotters.co.uk

Ceramatech Ltd
Units 16 & 17 Frontier Works
33 Queen Street
Tottenham North
London N17 8JA
Tel: 0208 885 4492
www.ceramatech.co.uk

CTM Potters Supplies
Unit 10A, Mill Park Industrial Estate
White Cross Road
Woodbury Salterton
EX5 1EL
Tel: 01395 233077
Web:
admin@ctmpotterssupplies.co.uk

Potclays Ltd.
Brick Kiln Lane
Etruria
Stoke-on-Trent
ST4 7BP
Tel: 01782 219 816
www.potclays.co.uk

Potters Connection Ltd.
PO Box 3079
Stoke-on-Trent
ST4 9FW
Tel: 0782 598 729
www.pottersconnection.co.uk

Scarva Pottery Supplies
Unit 20
Scarva Road Industrial Estate
Banbridge
Co. Down BT32 3QD
Northern Ireland
048 40669699
www.scarvapottery.com

Valentine Clays Ltd
The Sliphouse
18-22 Chell Street
Hanley
Stoke-on-Trent
ST1 6BA
01782 271 200
Web:
www.valentineclays.co.uk

Canada

Digitalfire Corporation:
www.digitalfire.com
Sells glaze-formulation software package called Insight.

Tuckers Pottery Supplies Inc.
15 West Pearce Street
Richmond Hill
Ontario, L4B1 H6
Canada
Tel: (800) 304-6185
Web:
www.tuckerspottery.com

USA

American Ceramic Supply Company
2442 Ludelle Street
Fort Worth
Texas 76105
Tel: (817) 535-2651
www.americanceramics.com

American Clay Art Company (Amaco)
6060 Guion Road
Indianapolis, IN 46254
USA
Tel: (800) 374-1600
www.amaco.com

Axner Pottery and Ceramic Supplies
490 Kane Court
Oviedo, FL 32765
USA
Tel: (800) 843-7057
www.axner.com

Bailey Ceramic Supplies
PO Box 1577
Kingston, NY 12402
USA
Tel: (845) 339-3721
www.baileypottery.com

Campbell's Ceramic Supply:
4231 Carolina Ave.
Richmond
Virginia 23222
www.claysupply.com

Continental Clay Company
1101 Stinson Blvd. NE
Minneapolis, MN 55413
Tel: (612) 331-9332 (local)
www.continentalclay.com

Frog Pond Pottery
PO Box 88
Pocopson, PA 15242-0240
Tel (412) 276 6333
www.frogpondpottery.com
Sells glaze-formulation software package called Glazemaster.

Highwater Clays
600 Riverside Drive
Asheville, NC 28801
Tel: 828.252.6033
www.highwaterclays.com
Sells glaze-formulation software and Mastering Cone 6 Glaze book.

Laguna Clay Company
1440 Lomitas Avenue
City of Industry
CA 91746, USA
Tel: (800) 452-4862
www.lagunaclay.com

Standard Clay Company
(online shop)
PO Box 16240
Pittsburgh, PA 15242-0240
Tel: (412) 276-6333
www.standardceramic.com

Glossary

Anneal: to slow-cool a kiln.

Ball clay: a secondary clay distinguished by its relatively small particle size and high iron content.

Base glaze: a glaze without added colourants or suspending agents.

Bisque-fire: firing dry clay pieces in a kiln in order to vitrify them with the intention of making the glazing process easier.

Bisque ware: pieces that have been bisque-fired.

Blebbing/bloating: bubbles that appear in a clay during firing as a result of overheating or firing too fast.

Clay: in its pure form, a material made up of alumina, silica and chemically bound water.

Cone: 1. a small cone-shaped piece of clay that softens and melts at a specific 'cone' value. 2. a numbered value that indicates a specific amount of heat work.

Cone pack: a group of cones clustered together in a wad of clay.

Crawling: when a glaze pulls away from an area on a pot during a firing.

Crystalline glaze: a glaze with a surface broken up with crystals. Macro-crystalline glazes have individual crystals that can be seen with the naked eye; micro-crystalline glazes usually have a matt surface and individual crystals can be seen with a microscope.

Cullet: ground-up window or bottle glass.

Draw-rings: small rings of clay that can be removed (using an iron bar) from a kiln during a firing.

Dunting: cracking of pottery caused by the stresses of heating and cooling.

Engobe: see 'Slip' definition 1.

Feldspar: a type of rock containing silica, alumina and any number of other oxides.

Firebrick: bricks designed to withstand high temperatures.

Firing schedule: the programme a kiln follows during a firing, including temperature changes and rate of temperature increase.

Flocculation: small particles gathering together into clumps.

Flux: an ingredient in a glaze or clay body that upon heating lowers the melting temperature of other ingredients.

Frit: a ground-up glass designed specifically for high-temperature applications.

Greenware: pieces that are dry but unfired.

Grog: fired clay that has been crushed into bits.

Heatwork: the amount of heat energy applied over time to objects in a kiln.

Kaolin: a primary clay distinguished by its relatively large particle size and the absence of iron.

Kiln furniture: the posts, bricks and shelves used inside a kiln to support the ware.

Kiln wash: a thin layer of refractory material applied to the surfaces of kiln furniture to keep glazes and soda or salt fumes from sticking.

Leatherhard: clay that is firm but still pliable. If shaped like a slab, it can stand up yet still be easily carved.

Maiolica: a low-fire white glaze containing tin.

Mason stains: manufactured colourants that have been fired (like a frit) to combine various raw colouring agents.

Molochite: a porcelain grog.

MSDS Sheets: Material Safety Data Sheets that list information about chemicals and their hazards.

Oxide: a molecule made from the combination of an oxygen atom and one or more other atoms.

Pinholes: small gaps in a finished glaze surface caused by gases escaping from the clay during the firing.

Plasticity: a characteristic of clay determined by the average particle size in a given clay. Very plastic clays will have small particles and be very sticky and flexible. Non-plastic clays will have larger particles, will be less sticky and will tend to crack and crumble.

Pug mill: a machine used to blend wet clays together. A de-airing pug mill has a vacuum-pump attachment that removes trapped air bubbles from the clay, thereby reducing or eliminating the need for wedging.

Pyrometer: a high-temperature thermometer.

Reduction: the process of reducing the amount of oxygen in a fuel-burning kiln.

Refractory: a term indicating the extent to which a material can resist change as a result of heating.

Saggar: a protective shield or container used to reduced thermal shock during a firing.

Single firing: the practice of firing pieces once, applying glazes to the wet or dry pieces but not bisque firing.

Slake: the natural process that occurs when completely dry clay is rewetted: the dry clay disintegrates as the water penetrates.

Slip: 1. a thick liquid coloured clay used to decorate by applying direct to a piece (leatherhard or bisque), and sometimes over a glaze. 2. a liquid clay used when casting shapes in moulds. 3. a thin liquid clay used to help attach pieces of leatherhard clay together (as in 'scoring and slipping').

Soaking: (in a kiln) means holding the temperature at a certain level for a specific length of time.

Source: as it pertains to glaze making, the compounds 'sourced' by a given ingredient are the ones that form part of the glaze after firing. Since firing rearranges atoms in many materials, the sourced compounds (mostly oxides) are sometimes quite different from the compounds found in the raw ingredient.

Underglaze: see 'Slip' definition 1.

Vitrification: the partial melting of oxides in a clay body, rendering it impervious to liquids.

Wadding: refractory material used in wood and soda or salt firings to prevent ware from sticking together or to kiln furniture.

Ware: pieces made by clay artists.

Wash: a thin layer of a colourant applied for decoration as a very dilute mixture with water, usually by brushing, sponging or spraying directly onto bisqueware.

Wax resist: a masking technique that involves applying a wax to a piece prior to the application of a glaze.

Wedging: a method of pushing soft clay that merges it, to expel trapped air bubbles and encourage the mixing of ingredients.

Zircopax: trade name for zirconium silicate, an opacifier.

Index